T0329141

Margin Trading from A to Z

Founded in 1807, John Wiley & Sons is the oldest independent publishing company in the United States. With offices in North America, Europe, Australia and Asia, Wiley is globally committed to developing and marketing print and electronic products and services for our customers' professional and personal knowledge and understanding.

The Wiley Trading series features books by traders who have survived the market's ever changing temperament and have prospered—some by reinventing systems, others by getting back to basics. Whether a novice trader, professional or somewhere in-between, these books will provide the advice and strategies needed to prosper today and well into the future.

For a list of available titles, visit our Web site at www.WileyFinance.com.

Margin Trading from A to Z

A Complete Guide to Borrowing, Investing, and Regulation

MICHAEL T. CURLEY

WILEY

John Wiley & Sons, Inc.

Published by John Wiley & Sons, Inc., Hoboken, New Jersey
Published simultaneously in Canada

For general information on our other products and services or for technical support, please contact our Customer Care Department within the United States at (800) 762-2974, outside the United States at (317) 572-3993 or fax (317) 572-4002.

Wiley also publishes its books in a variety of electronic formats. Some content that appears in print may not be available in electronic formats. For more information about Wiley products, visit our web site at www.wiley.com.

Library of Congress Cataloging-in-Publication Data:

Curley, Michael T.
  Margin trading from A to Z : a complete guide to borrowing, investing, and regulation / Michael T. Curley.
      p. cm.
  Includes bibliographical references and index.
  ISBN 978-0-470-17394-7 (cloth : alk. paper) 978-1-119-10851-1 (paperback)
1. Margin accounts–United States. 2. Margins (Security trading)–United States.
  I. Title.
HG6041.C84 2008
332.63'2280973–dc22

                                                                        2007038098

10 9 8 7 6 5 4 3 2 1

This book is dedicated to all the men and women who toil in the back offices of the financial community. The work is hard, the compensation low, and the recognition minute. However, without you, this industry could not survive.

Thanks to you all!

Contents

Preface

Trading on margin has taken an unfair and unwarranted amount of abuse. Purchasing securities on margin is nothing more than purchasing securities on credit. Credit is not evil or bad and, if properly used, can be an extremely profitable means of investing.

If I told you that I had just purchased a house and paid for it in full, I am sure you would be surprised, because this is not the normal procedure for purchasing a house. Most people react to this statement by saying that (1) a house is a huge purchase requiring financing (true) and (2) there is no risk—real estate always increases in value (false).

I would be negligent not to tell you that any credit purchase of stocks, bonds, real estate, furniture, fixtures, and so on involves a degree of risk. However, a cash purchase in full of the same items involves the same degree of risk. The value of items purchased, whether financed or paid for in full, can decline, giving you a loss. Real estate prices have dropped substantially in certain geographical areas, areas that have experienced a decline in jobs and increased unemployment; a decline in real estate value usually accompanies it. The real estate decline affected houses being financed with a mortgage as well as those that were fully paid.

The first false notion one must discard is the idea that debt is bad. It is not. Borrowed funds used properly can result in considerable profits. The term *leveraged buyout* is very popular right now on Wall Street. It is nothing more than one company taking over another company with borrowed funds. Our economy and our standard of living as we know it today would not exist without credit.

The obvious fact in purchasing securities on credit, with the current requirements at 50 percent, is that one can purchase twice as much in a margin account as in a cash account. Consequently, if one purchases $10,000 worth of securities in a cash account and that security doubles in value, one has a profit of $10,000. The same $10,000 in a margin account enables one to purchase $20,000 in securities. Should these securities double in value, the profit is $20,000. That, in essence, is the principle behind margin trading.

Often, the complaint is voiced that an additional expense is involved in margin trading, because the broker charges interest on the money he or she is financing. And that is absolutely true. However, since one can purchase twice as many securities, twice as many dividends are available to offset a good portion of the interest charged.

A margin account can also be used to obtain financing for purposes other than buying and selling securities. Assume a customer has $60,000 in market value of listed securities and wants to buy a new car with a total sticker price of $27,000. Depositing these securities into a margin account, the broker is permitted to finance 50 percent, or $30,000. In this case, the customer has purchased his or her car and still maintained ownership of the securities. Interest charged by the broker is approximately the same as that charged by a bank for an auto loan. The advantage of the margin account is that the client does not have to make monthly payments to pay off the loan. The loan may be paid off at any time or can stay open indefinitely, provided the collateral is sufficient to meet the minimum maintenance requirement (this is discussed in detail in the text). In addition, the bank loan requires the automobile as collateral. The bank can thus dictate what kind of insurance must be purchased, whether alarms must be installed, and so on. However, with the margin account the loan is tied to the securities deposited and has nothing to do with the car.

While most margin accounts are longstanding accounts, many are opened and subsequently closed in a relatively short period of time. This is particularly true around April 15th of each year, when tax payments are due. Many times, securities are deposited and loans taken, the proceeds of which are used for the payment of taxes. Often these accounts are paid off and closed out relatively quickly.

At this point, a few comments should be made about margin trading risk. However, I first shall allay some of the misconceptions regarding two major crashes, October 29, 1929, and October 19, 1987.

One often hears that the 1929 crash was caused by margin trading. Although margin accounts were a factor, many other factors also came into play. To begin with, prior to the crash, no hard and fast margin requirements existed. The New York Stock Exchange had a suggested margin requirement of 20 percent. However, more often than not, customers were trading on 10 percent and in some cases 5 percent margin. This is clearly a case of too much credit. The sharp decline left many accounts in a deficit or close to no equity, forcing a liquidation. This has long since been rectified by the establishment of initial requirements (currently of 50 percent) and minimum maintenance requirements (currently 25 percent). As you can see, requirements are substantially higher now than in 1929.

The crash on October 19, 1987, was quite different. The stock market had changed substantially from 1929. Not only had the volume and the number of shares available increased, but new products had been introduced, such as equity options, broad-based index options, futures hedging strategies, program trading, and so-called *naked* writing of options, which can, at least in theory, result in unlimited loss.

Congress appointed a committee to look into the crash and come up with some suggestions to prevent a recurrence. As a result, margin requirements were increased on equity options and narrow- and broad-based index options, and new restrictions on program trading were implemented. No suggestion was made to increase either initial margin requirement of 50 percent or maintenance requirement of 25 percent.

I know some will say, what about the crash in 2000? In all fairness, the decline starting in 2000 and continuing for several years was a slow deterioration of the market value of securities, particularly the tech stocks. Fortunes were lost: From a peak of $260 billion, total debit balances dropped to a low of $165 billion. As of this writing, debit balances have returned to $233 billion.

As previously stated, there is risk in any investment. However, with knowledge of the product, diversification, and constant monitoring, risk can be greatly reduced. Certainly, there is nothing new in these concepts. However, an essential ingredient that is often overlooked is a thorough understanding of the vehicle (the margin account), which accommodates the purchasing and carrying of securities on margin. As of this writing, approximately 5,000,000 margin accounts exist, with debit balances in excess of $233 billion. The vast majority of these accounts are individual customers rather than institutional investors. I would venture to say that only a small percentage of customers who have margin accounts and the registered representatives servicing these accounts could get a passing grade on the exam at the back of this book.

Michael T. Curley

About the Author

M ichael T. Curley has over 50 years experience in the financial community including 15 years in the banking industry and 15 years in the brokerage industry. Mr. Curley began his career as a regulator with The New York Stock Exchange in the Division of Margin.

In 1974, Mr. Curley joined the faculty at The New York Institute of Finance. Since 1987, Mr. Curley has been a full-time financial trainer and consultant. Due to his extensive knowledge, he has served as an expert witness on numerous occasions.

Mr. Curley is a graduate of Adelphi University and lives with his wife in New York City.

Cash Accounts

M ost security transactions take place in the customer's cash account. Regulation T of the board of governors of the Federal Reserve System (the Fed)[1] states that funds sufficient for the purchase of the securities should be in the account prior to the purchase. In the event that funds are not on hand, there is an agreement between the broker and the customer that the customer will deposit the full cash payment "promptly."

Promptly is an important word. The Fed defines it to mean three (3) business days. Consequently, full cash payment should be received by the third business day—the settlement date. This would be an ideal or optimum situation, since the broker would be using the customer's money to pay for the purchase on the settlement date. The broker is required to pay the seller on the settlement date, whether or not the customer has paid for the purchase. If the customer has not paid by the settlement day, the broker would have to borrow from the bank, incurring an interest expense, which is not passed on to the customer.

Although the regulation states that payment should be received by the third business day, it goes one step further and states that payment must be received no later than the fifth (5th) business day. As you can see, while payment received on the fifth business day satisfies Regulation T, the broker has incurred an expense of two days' interest charged by the bank. (The interest rate charged the broker by the bank is known as the broker's *call rate.*)

---

[1]See Appendix A for a detailed discussion of the Federal Reserve System.

What happens in the event payment is not received by the fifth business day?

1. In the event an exceptional circumstance exists—for example, the customer was called out of town unexpectedly or became ill—the broker may request an extension of time from one of the exchanges or the NASD.

   The extension of time is requested electronically, giving the customer's name, the quantity, description of the security purchased, total dollar amount involved, the reason for the delay, number of days requested, and the customer's Social Security number.

   The request for an extension of time is submitted to the exchange or the NASD. That is classified as the *designated examining authority* (DEA). If granted, the customer now has more time to pay. The maximum number of extensions that a customer can receive is five in any 12-month period.

2. Should payment not be received within the approved period, or if the extension was denied, the broker would be required to liquidate or sell out the customer's securities to pay for this purchase.

At this point, what has happened in the customer's account? The proceeds of the sale have been used to pay for the purchase. This is a violation of Regulation T, and the customer's account is frozen for the next 90 calendar days. The effect of this 90-day penalty is to require the customer to have sufficient funds on hand prior to any new purchase. No longer may the customer call the broker, purchase a security, and then send in a check in payment.

Keep in mind that the Federal Reserve is concerned with the amount of credit outstanding. The cash account is specifically designed for customers wishing to buy and pay in full for their securities. By buying and selling without full cash payment, the customer is, in effect, trading on 100 percent margin.

Regulation T also allows for an exception. Should a customer purchase a security one day and sell that very same security two days later, this customer's cash account would immediately become frozen for 90 calendar days. However, should the customer make full cash payment within five business days, the restriction is automatically lifted. The Federal Reserve's reasoning is that, while the customer did buy and sell before making full cash payment, full cash payment (not just the difference between the purchase and the sale) was eventually made within the prescribed time. Should payment be received after the fifth business day, the broker must make written application to an exchange or NASD to have the freeze lifted.

SALE OF SECURITIES

The sale of a security in the customer's cash account has requirements similar to those for a purchase.

The securities to be sold should be held in the customer's account (long), or there must be an agreement that the customer will deliver the security "promptly." Again, *promptly* is defined as three business days. This will enable the broker to deliver the security to the buying broker and obtain the payments.

Until January 15, 1973, the final settlement of the sale of a security was vague at best. Effective that date, the Securities Exchange Act of 1934 was amended to include Rule 15c 3–3-(M) and (N). This rule now requires that the sold securities be delivered no later than ten (10) business days after settlement. Should an exceptional circumstance arise, an extension of time may be requested from a national securities exchange or association such as the NASD. At the expiration of the extension, if the security is still not delivered, the broker is required to buy in the security. Unlike the purchase side, this would not freeze the account. However, many brokerage firms impose a 90-day freeze in this situation. This is not a Regulation T requirement, but it is commonly known as a *house requirement*.

PAYING FOR SECURITIES BY THE SALE OF OTHER SECURITIES

If a security is to be paid for by the sale of another security, the sale should take place in time for sufficient funds to be on hand by the settlement date. Therefore, the purchase and the sale should be completed the same day.

The question now arises: What happens if a customer buys a security on day one and sells another security to pay for that purchase on day three? If such a transaction happened occasionally, there would be no problem. However, this transaction will cost the broker two days' interest, since the purchase transaction will settle two days before the funds become available. In addition, if such transactions occur with any degree of regularity, many firms, while not required to freeze the account for 90 days, will impose such a restriction as a house policy. Infractions of this type should be monitored by the margin clerks and should be brought to management's attention for corrective action. Keep in mind that these transactions are costly because of the interest being charged.

Normal settlement for equity and debt (exclusive of U.S. government obligations) instruments is three business days from the trade date (often referred to as a regular way trade basis or settlement). On occasion, if an individual requires immediate funds, such an arrangement may be accomplished by a cash sale. Such sales settle on the same day at 2:30 P.M. Any trade executed at 2:00 P.M. or later settles 30 minutes after the trade.

DELIVERY AGAINST PAYMENT

Another type of transaction also takes place in the customer's cash account—the C.O.D. (cash on delivery) or D.V.P. (delivery versus payment). This transaction is normally reserved for large institutional customers. However, any account could, at least in theory, transact business on this basis. The procedure works as follows.

When a customer purchases a security, the security is physically delivered to the customer, and the customer then pays for the purchase. Two conditions are attached to such a transaction. First, the customer must advise the broker prior to the purchase that the method of payment is going to be *delivery versus payment,* and the broker must agree to the procedure. Second, in the event the broker is unable to obtain the security to accomplish delivery, the broker has up to 35 calendar days to complete the delivery. That is, if the broker is unable to obtain the security by the fifth business day, the broker is not obligated to liquidate the customer's account or obtain an extension of time. The broker has 35 calendar days from the trade date to accomplish delivery.

As a matter of information, transactions of this type normally settle on the third business day. This is so for two reasons. First, should delivery not be accomplished promptly, a good chance exists that the broker has part, but not all, of the securities for delivery. Consequently, the broker has paid for some of the securities out of his or her own pocket, financed by a bank. Since a large portion of the broker's transactions are of this sort, special emphasis is placed on this area. Separate sections in the margin department only work on these types of transactions, ensuring proper delivery instructions to the cashiers department. Second, there is an organization known as Depository Trust Clearing Corp. (DTCC) that has immobilized many stock certificates, eliminating the physical movement of certificates from broker to bank or to another broker.

Most institutional customers set up what are called *standing instructions* to deliver versus payment to a particular agent (usually a bank). The bank accepting the securities assigns an individual to handle and process the securities for this account. Anytime the institutional customer makes a purchase, a duplicate confirmation is sent to the receiving bank so it can anticipate that 1,000 shares of IBM will be delivered on settlement versus $93,000. Upon delivery, the bank will pay the broker. Depository Trust Clearing Corp. established a service a number of years ago called Institutional Delivery System (ID System) that enables brokers/dealers to confirm and settle trades electronically. This process enables brokers to process the huge volume of today.

Should the receiving agent be another broker, then upon delivery of the security, the receiving broker must present the delivering broker with a free funds letter. This letter merely states that the funds for payment of this purchase do not represent the proceeds of the sale of the security. Should the delivering broker not obtain this letter, the account must be frozen for 90 calendar days. As you can see, it would be extremely easy to buy using one broker and then sell using another and issue instructions for delivery versus payment. In order to prevent what is commonly referred to as *free riding*, a *free funds letter* must be obtained.

On occasion, delivery of securities is made and the delivery is rejected (DK'd). The receiving agent must attach a form called a DK (*don't know*) notice and advise the delivering party of the reason for rejection—for example, delivery versus wrong amount of money, securities not in good delivery form, a mutilated coupon, or no knowledge of the trade. When this occurs, the 35-day period is immediately canceled and you must request an extension of time. The New York Stock Exchange will normally grant you two days to clear up this problem.

As previously mentioned, C.O.D. and D.V.P. transactions are normally reserved for institutional clients such as pension plans, banks, broker/dealers, insurance companies, charitable and other not for profit companies, hedge funds, and investment companies. As you can imagine, customers such as these can and often are large organizations trading millions of dollars per transaction.

As these types of transactions grew over the years, additional regulatory requirements were needed. Consequently, effective June 7, 1971, The New York Stock Exchange adopted Rule 387 governing C.O.D./D.V.P./P.O.D. (payment on delivery).

Fortunately, this particular rule is very straightforward and easy to understand. The following is Rule 387 in its entirety:

COD Orders

Rule 387. (a) No member or member organization shall accept an order from a customer pursuant to an arrangement whereby payment for securities purchased or delivery of securities sold is to be made to or by an agent of the customer unless all of the following procedures are followed:

1. *The member or member organization shall have received from the customer prior to or at the time of accepting the order, the name and address of the agent and the name and account number of the customer on file with the agent.*

2. *Each order accepted from the customer pursuant to such an arrangement has noted thereon the fact that it is a payment on delivery (POD) or collect on delivery (COD) transaction.*

3. *The member or member organization delivers to the customer a confirmation, or all relevant data customarily contained in a confirmation with respect to the execution of the order, in whole or in part, not later than the close of business on the next business day after such execution, and*

4. *The member organization has obtained an agreement from the customer that the customer will furnish his agent instructions with respect to the receipt or delivery of the securities involved in the transaction promptly upon receipt by the customer of each confirmation, or the relevant data as to each execution, relating to such order (even though such execution represents the purchase or sale of only a part of the order), and that in any event the customer will assure that such instructions are delivered to his agent no later than:*

   i. *in the case of a purchase by the customer where the agent is to receive the securities against payment (COD), the close of business on the second business day after the date of execution of the trade as to which the particular confirmation relates; or*

   ii. *in the case of a sale by the customer where the agent is to deliver the securities against payment (POD), the close of business on the first business day after the date of execution of the trade as to which the particular confirmation relates.*

5. *The facilities of a Clearing Agency shall be utilized for the book-entry settlement of all depository eligible transactions.*

EMPLOYEE STOCK OPTIONS

A popular compensation for executives, as well as other employees, is the issuance of stock options. Most employee stock options are in fact exercised in the customer's margin account, enabling the customer to finance a portion of the cost of exercising such option. However, employee stock options may be exercised in the customer's cash account. The customer must finance 100 percent of the transaction.

CHAPTER ONE QUESTIONS

1. Under Regulation T a purchase in a cash account must be paid for:
   a. by the settlement date.
   b. within five business days.
   c. within seven calendar days.
   d. within three business days.

2. A cash account becomes frozen for 90 calendar days when a customer:
   a. pays for a purchase after the settlement date.
   b. sells a security and delivers it after the seventh business day.
   c. has been granted more than five extensions of time.
   d. buys a security and sells the same security and has not paid for it.

3. The Securities Act of 1934 requires a customer to deliver sold securities to the broker no later than:
   a. 10 calendar days after trade date.
   b. 10 business days after settlement date.
   c. 35 calendar days.
   d. 90 calendar days.

4. In order to qualify for the 35-day provision for a C.O.D. or D.V.P. transaction under Regulation T, the customer must issue instructions prior to the trade and:
   a. the securities cannot be obtained by the broker for delivery.
   b. request permission from the NYSE.
   c. request delivery after settlement date.
   d. there is no other requirement.

5. Extension of time may be requested from which organization?
   a. the Federal Reserve
   b. the NYSE
   c. the SEC
   d. all of the above

6. Extension of time should be requested:
   a. on the settlement date.
   b. on the seventh calendar day.
   c. on the fifth business day after the trade date.
   d. as soon as you know there will be a delay in payment.

7. A broker may remove a 90-day freeze if:
   a. the loss incurred is deposited by the seventh business day.
   b. under no circumstances.
   c. full cash payment is received by the fifth business day after purchase.
   d. the broker makes written application to the Federal Reserve Bank.

8. A regular way basis or settlement means the trade settles:
   a. 90 calendar days later.
   b. 35 calendar days later.
   c. on the seventh business day.
   d. on the third business day.

9. When a delivery of securities is DK'd, the rejecting broker must:
   a. advise the registered representative.
   b. advise the delivery broker why the item is being DK'd.
   c. cancel the trade.
   d. accept delivery if it is for less than $10,000.

10. A cash trade settles:
   a. on the fifth business day.
   b. the same day.
   c. on the seventh business day.
   d. at 2:30 P.M. on the next business day.

CHAPTER 2

Initial Federal Margin Requirements

A *margin* transaction is essentially a credit transaction where the customer pays a portion of the purchase and the broker finances the balance. The amount that the broker is permitted to finance is controlled by the board of governors of the Federal Reserve under Regulation T. Currently, the broker is permitted to finance 50 percent of the purchase price (the current market value). This amount is commonly referred to as the *Fed requirement*, *Regulation T requirement*, or the *initial requirement*.

PURCHASES

Marginable securities are defined by Regulation T as

1. Any security registered or having unlisted trading privileges on a national securities exchange;
2. After January 1, 1999, any security listed on the Nasdaq Stock Market;
3. Any non-equity security;
4. Any security issued by either an open-end investment company or unit investment trust which is registered under section 8 of the Investment Company Act of 1940 (15 U.S.C. 80a–8);
5. Any foreign margin stock;

6. Any debt security convertible into a margin security;
7. Until January 1, 1999, any OTC margin stock; or
8. Until January 1, 1999, any OTC security designated as qualified for trading in the national market system under a designation plan approved by the Securities and Exchange Commission (NMS security) (Regulation T: Credit by Brokers and Dealers, section 220.2).

What happens when a customer purchases a security in a margin account? Any time a customer purchases securities in a margin account, the market value of the account is increased by the purchase, and so is the debit balance. There are no exceptions. It is this increase in the customer's debit balance that causes what is commonly referred to as a *T call* or a *Fed call*. Remember that the Federal Reserve requires a deposit of 50 percent of the purchase price of the security. The required margin deposit is due promptly. Prompt payment of the T or Fed call means the third business day and no later than the fifth business day. Requests for extensions are treated the same for both cash and margin transactions.

Suppose a customer purchases 100 shares of ABC for $10,000. (For illustration purposes, commissions and interest charges have been eliminated.)

Market value	$10,000
Debit balance	10,000

Since this account started off with a zero balance, the market value is simply the price of the ABC shares. The debit balance represents the amount of money the customer owes the broker. At this point, the customer purchased $10,000 in securities and has not yet deposited the money.

The customer would then be issued a Fed call for $5,000, or 50 percent of the market value of the ABC shares. The actual format of the Fed call will vary from brokerage firm to brokerage firm. Some will have a very official-looking request giving the details of the transaction; others use a simple phone call from the broker.

In any event, assume in our case that the customer promptly deposits the required margin of $5,000. The account now looks like this:

Market value	$10,000
Debit balance	5,000
Equity	5,000

The money that the customer deposits reduces the debit balance by the amount of the deposit. Any time money is deposited into a margin account, the debit balance is reduced by the amount of the deposit.

Equity represents the customer's ownership in the account. If the securities were sold and all debts were paid ($5,000 in our example), $5,000 would be left. This last $5,000 represents equity. Equity is computed by subtracting the debit balance from the current market value.

Why do people buy on margin? They are employing *financial leverage*. If you buy $5,000 in securities paying cash, and the security doubles in value, you have earned a $5,000 profit. That same $5,000 could be used by you to purchase $10,000 on margin. If that security doubles, you will have earned a $10,000 profit, or twice as much. That, of course, is the bright side of margin buying. The dark side is that leverage on margin buying works both ways. With the margin account you can either double your gains or double your losses.

Getting back to our example, the customer's account is as follows:

Market value	$10,000
Debit balance	5,000
Equity	5,000

Let's assume that the value of the ABC shares increases to $12,000. The account would now look like this:

Market value	$12,000
Debit balance	5,000
Equity	7,000

The market value changed to reflect the increase or the current market value. The debit balance remains unchanged. Keep in mind that the debit balance is the amount of money the customer owes the broker. There was no additional loan or extension of credit. Also note that the customer's equity changed in response to the increase in market value:

$$\text{Equity} = \text{Market value} - \text{Debit balance}$$

Now we will make our first margin computation. Remember, you are concerned with current market value versus current Regulation T requirement.

Current market value	$12,000
Current Fed requirement	50%

Margin clerks have used the following tool for years to assist them in making the various margin computations:

Draw a large "T" as shown, putting requirement (Req.) on one side and equity (Eq.) on the other. Now you can take 50 percent of the current market value to get the Regulation T requirement.

$$\$12,000 \times 50\% = \$6,000 \text{ (the current requirement)}$$

Now, find the equity.

$$\text{Market value} - \text{Debit balance} = \text{Equity}$$
$$\$12,000 - \$5,000 = \$7,000$$

The equity is $7,000

Req.	Eq.
$6,000	$7,000

Now, subtract the requirement from the equity;

Req.	Eq.	
$6,000	$7,000	
	6,000	
	$1,000	excess over Reg. T

The $1,000 is known as *excess over Regulation T*. Excess means extra, something not required. Question: If it is extra or not required, may I have it? The answer is yes.

Now, if the customer requests and receives a check for the $1,000, the account will appear as follows:

Market value	$12,000
Debit balance	6,000
Equity	6,000

Sending the customer $1,000 increases the debit balance. This is because the broker loaned the customer an additional $1,000 based on the current value of the collateral, which is now worth $12,000. This additional $1,000 loan is permissible under Regulation T.

When referring to margin and margin accounts, we often think of a two-sided account. On one side, the customer side, there is a requirement to have 50 percent of the market value on deposit. On the other side, the broker side, the potential exists to lend the customer up to 50 percent of the market value. Therefore, in the previous example the broker was able to and did lend the customer an additional $1,000.

As stated earlier, any time money is *deposited* into the customer's account, regardless of the reason, the debit balance is *decreased*. It would stand to reason, then, that any time funds are *withdrawn*, the debit balance would be *increased* by that amount. In our example, the customer withdrew $1,000; consequently, the debit balance was increased by the amount of the withdrawal.

Although a withdrawal of $1,000 is permissible, the $1,000 excess can also be converted into *buying power*. Buying power means the amount of securities you can purchase without depositing any additional funds. With a 50 percent Regulation T requirement, all you do to find the buying power is double the excess (multiply by 2):

Req.	**Eq.**	
$6,000	$7,000	
	6,000	
	$1,000	excess over Reg. T
	×2	
	$2,000	buying power

If the customer purchased $2,000 of listed securities in the account, it will appear as follows:

Market value	$14,000
Debit balance	7,000
Equity	7,000

The market value increased by the value of the securities purchased—$2,000. Also, the debit balance was increased by the full purchase price. Why? Because the customer just purchased securities valued at $2,000 and has not paid for them. Keep in mind that there is another side to the transaction—someone sold the customer $2,000 worth of securities. If the customer did not pay for them, the broker would have to finance the entire purchase. Therefore, this additional loan is reflected as an increase in the customer's debit balance in this situation. The customer used the excess equity and did not have to make a deposit in the account. As a result of this transaction, the account is now at exactly 50 percent.

Any additional purchases at this point would require the necessary 50 percent deposit. Should this customer purchase another $5,000 in listed securities, the account would appear as follows:

Market value	$19,000
Debit balance	12,000
Equity	7,000

A Reg. T call for 50 percent of $5,000 ($2,500) would be issued and should be answered promptly (three business days). If the customer deposits the funds within the prescribed time, the margin account would now appear as follows:

Market value	$19,000
Debit balance	9,500
Equity	9,500

Again, funds were received into the account; therefore, the equity was increased and the debit balance was reduced by the deposited amount.

The Federal Reserve's requirement of 50 percent is also known as an *initial* requirement and would not come into effect again until there was an additional purchase. This purchase would, of course, trigger a new initial requirement of 50 percent of the purchase price.

Up to this point, we have discussed only the effects on a margin account when the price of the securities increases in market value. Excess is created and buying power is established. What happens when there is a decline in market value?

If the market value were to decline to $17,000, the account would change accordingly:

Market value	$17,000
Debit balance	9,500
Equity	7,500

The market value changed to reflect the decrease in the price of the securities. The debit balance remains unchanged—the client still owes the broker $9,500. The equity decreased in response to the decrease in market value. Remember:

$$\text{Equity} = \text{Market value} - \text{Debit balance}$$

The margin account is now known as a *restricted margin account*. This is not to be confused with a cash account on a 90-day restriction or freeze. A restricted margin account means that the customer's equity is below the current Federal Reserve margin requirement of 50 percent. The restriction actually applies to the broker, who may not lend the customer any additional funds. In our account, the Regulation T requirement is

$$50\% \times \$17,000 = \$8,500$$

yet the current equity is only $7,500.

Req.	Eq.
$8,500	$7,500

In this case, the requirement exceeds the equity in the customer's account.

Does this mean that the customer is prohibited from purchasing additional securities? Absolutely not. Most active margin accounts are, in fact, restricted margin accounts. The margin trader may buy additional securities with any excess over Regulation T. Therefore, should the market have a sell-off, the market value would go down, reducing the trader's equity and thereby restricting the account. A restricted margin account carries no bad connotation. The broker merely cannot lend the customer additional funds as the account stands. Any new purchases will require a 50 percent deposit, and the broker may extend credit for these new purchases. In the event this customer purchases additional securities of $6,000, the account would appear as follows:

Market value	$23,000 (increased by $6,000)
Debit balance	15,500 (increased by $6,000)
Equity	7,500 (unchanged)

The customer would get a Reg. T call for 50 percent of the purchase price ($3,000). When the customer deposits the required $3,000 promptly, the account would change to:

Market value	$23,000 (unchanged)
Debit balance	12,500 (decreased by $3,000)
Equity	10,500 (increased by $3,000)

After the deposit of the required margin, this account is still classified as a restricted margin account. It is not necessary to bring the entire account back up to 50 percent margin. The customer was required only to deposit 50 percent of the last purchase.

SALES

Thus far, our examples and discussion have been about purchases. Sales of securities in a margin account are the exact opposite of purchases.

Let's go back to our margin account:

Market value	$23,000
Debit balance	12,500
Equity	10,500

If this customer sold $5,000 of securities, the market value would be reduced by the proceeds of sale, $5,000. The debit balance would also be reduced by $5,000. The debit balance is reduced by the full amount, because the broker actually received the proceeds of sale, since the broker is holding the securities as collateral. Although the customer is the beneficial owner of the securities, they are usually held in the name of the broker or the broker's nominee (street name).

When a sale of securities occurs, 50 percent of the proceeds of the sale may be released to the customer (the reverse of a purchase requiring a deposit).

Here is the customer's account after the sale but prior to the release of any of the proceeds:

Market value	$18,000
Debit balance	7,500
Equity	10,500

If the customer was sent a check for $2,500, 50% of $5,000, the account would change to:

Market value	$18,000
Debit balance	10,000
Equity	8,000

As previously stated, any time money comes into the margin account, the debit balance is reduced. Any time money leaves the account, the debit balance is increased. A further look at this account also reveals that after the permissible withdrawal, the margin account is still classified as a restricted margin account.

Fifty percent of market value is $9,000. The customer's equity is only $8,000.

Req.	Eq.
$9,000	$8,000

MEETING A MARGIN CALL

Up to this point, the customer has met the Fed or Reg. T calls by depositing money. This is quite common. However, there are other methods of meeting a margin call.

In addition to having a 50 percent requirement on purchases, listed and marginable securities have *loan value*. If a customer deposited fully paid for marginable securities, the broker would be permitted to lend the customer 50 percent of their current market value. Therefore, a Reg. T call could be satisfied with a deposit of securities valued at two times the call.

Suppose our customer now makes an additional purchase of $7,000. The account would look like this:

Market value	$25,000
Debit balance	17,000
Equity	8,000

There would be an outstanding Reg. T call of $3,500. The customer could deposit marginable securities worth $7,000 to satisfy the Reg. T call (50% × $7,000 = $3,500).

After the deposit of the securities, the account would now look like this:

Market value	$32,000
Debit balance	17,000
Equity	15,000

The market value and the equity increased by the value of securities deposited, but no change was made to the customer's debit balance. Deposits of securities will only affect the market value and equity in an account. The debit balance is the amount owed to the broker and will be reduced only by depositing monies.

Another way of meeting a margin call is through the sale of other securities. As was the case in the cash account, in a margin account sales

of securities to pay for purchases should be placed on the same day, so
that the settlement dates coincide. If a customer purchases $7,000 and sells
$7,000 of securities on the same day, no change occurs in the customer ac-
count. However, it is unusual to come out exactly even. Often, there is a
slight difference. If there were a purchase of $7,500 and a sale of $7,300,
the purchase would exceed the sale by $200, requiring a T call of $100, or
50 percent of the difference. In this regard, Regulation T has the provision
that calls for $1,000 or less may be waived at the option of the broker. In
the event the sale takes place after the trade date of the purchase, the account is said to be meeting the margin call by *liquidation*. The NYSE has
stated through interpretation of its margin rules that "a practice of meeting margin calls by liquidation is prohibited." What constitutes *a practice*?
This is subject to interpretation based on the number of transactions the
customer makes.

The last way to meet a Reg. T call, and perhaps the least likely to occur,
is by market appreciation. Here is an example:

Market value	$100,000
Debit balance	52,000
Equity	48,000
Buy 100 ABC at	2,000

This triggers a Reg. T call of $1,000.
Here is the margin account after purchase:

Market value	$102,000
Debit balance	54,000
Equity	48,000

Should the market value of the margin account increase between the
trade date and settlement date (three business days) to $108,000 or more,
the $1,000 Reg. T margin call will be considered answered. With the market
value at $108,000 and the debit at $54,000, equity would be at exactly 50
percent, requiring no additional funds.

		Req.	**Eq.**
Market value	$108,000	$54,000	$54,000
Debit balance	54,000		
Equity	54,000		

To summarize, there are four ways to meet a Reg. T margin call:

1. Deposit the required funds.
2. Sell a security of equal or greater value than the security purchased.

3. Deposit securities having loan value equal to or greater than the margin call.

4. Benefit from market appreciation.

CHAPTER TWO QUESTIONS

1. Excess over Regulation T is:

   a. the amount that is required as a result of purchases in a customer's margin account.

   b. the amount a broker may finance as a result of a purchase of listed securities.

   c. the amount of money in excess of Regulation T that may be withdrawn from the account or used to purchase additional securities.

   d. all of the above.

2. The amount of money that the broker finances is called:

   a. current market value.

   b. excess over Regulation T.

   c. equity.

   d. debit balance.

3. Loan value is:

   a. the market value of all securities in an account.

   b. the amount of the customer's debt.

   c. the amount of money that may be loaned to the customer based on the value of listed securities.

   d. a good faith deposit.

4. A regulation T call must be met within:

   a. seven business days after the trade date.

   b. five business days after the trade date.

   c. the next business day.

   d. 35 calendar days.

5. A Regulation T call may be answered by:

   a. a deposit of money.

   b. a deposit of securities with sufficient loan value.

   c. liquidation.

   d. all of the above.

6. The initial Regulation T requirement is 50 percent, and the account has a long market value of $40,000 and a debit balance of $12,500. What is the Regulation T excess?

   a. $750
   b. $7,500
   c. $10,000
   d. $15,000

7. Use the account information from question 6. What is the buying power in this account?

   a. $1,500
   b. none
   c. $15,000
   d. $20,000

8. The customer's account is as follows, and Regulation T is at 50 percent.

Market value	$25,000
Debit balance	15,000
Equity	10,000

   This account is:

   a. a cash account.
   b. a restricted margin account.
   c. in deficit.
   d. a restricted cash account.

9. Use the account information from question 8. The customer purchases $8,500 of listed securities. After the purchase, the debit balance will:

   a. remain the same.
   b. be $23,500.
   c. be $19,250.
   d. be $10,750.

10. (Same account as above) How much will this account will be on call for?

    a. $10,000
    b. $16,750
    c. $8,500
    d. $4,250

Initial and Minimum Maintenance Requirements

Thus far, we have discussed the initial requirements of the Federal Reserve Board. What happens after the margin account has been opened and the required margin is deposited? As far as the Federal Reserve is concerned, its job was finished when the initial requirement was set and satisfied. If the market value of the securities went to zero, it would be of no concern to the Federal Reserve. However, not only would the customer be in a precarious position, but so would the broker who is financing the transaction.

To prevent the broker from having an account become an unsecured debit, the NYSE as well as the regional exchanges and the NASD have established initial and minimum *maintenance* requirements.

The margin rules of the New York and regional stock exchanges and the NASD are similar. Further discussion of maintenance requirements will refer only to the NYSE rules.

INITIAL REQUIREMENTS

The initial equity requirement to open or trade in a margin account is $2,000. Therefore, a customer wishing to open an account using the maximum financing (50 percent) and the minimum initial deposit would have to purchase $4,000 market value of securities. The account would them look like this:

Market value	$4,000
Debit balance	2,000
Equity	2,000

Purchase of a lesser amount—say $3,000—would still require an initial deposit of $2,000, even though this exceeds the Regulation T requirement of 50 percent.

A purchase of $1,800 in a new margin account would require only $1,800. A broker would never ask a customer to deposit more than the full cost of the security.

The initial requirements of the NYSE are exactly that—initial requirements. The $2,000 does not have to be maintained. In our first example, the customer's account looked like this:

Market value	$4,000
Debit balance	2,000
Equity	2,000

If the market value declined to $3,000, the customer's account would appear thus:

Market value	$3,000
Debit balance	2,000
Equity	1,000

This account is in compliance with the NYSE rules and is in satisfactory condition. Although the equity is now below $2,000, this was occasioned by market activity and not by a withdrawal of funds. However, if this customer now wished to purchase $1,000 of listed securities, this transaction would be subject to the NYSE $2,000 requirement. The customer would, therefore, be required to deposit the full $1,000, as opposed to the $500 Regulation T requirement.

The customer's account after the purchase and $1,000 deposit would now appear as follows:

Market value	$4,000
Debit balance	2,000
Equity	2,000

HOUSE REQUIREMENTS

The rules of the NYSE and the Federal Reserve are minimum requirements. Brokers may (and most do) have house requirements in excess of the NYSE and Federal Reserve minimums. This is fine, as long as the house requirements are not lower than these minimum requirements. One firm that I know of has a house requirement of $250,000 to open a margin account. Obviously, this broker is interested in a select group of customers.

The balance of this chapter will explain in detail the NYSE minimum maintenance requirement on long positions (securities owned). Keep in mind that many firms have house requirements in excess of these minimums and, in fact, requirements vary from broker to broker.

NYSE MINIMUM MAINTENANCE REQUIREMENTS

The NYSE, in addition to the initial requirement, has a minimum maintenance requirement that the customer's equity in the account must be equal to at least 25 percent of the market value of the securities.

As an example, assume a customer purchases $10,000 of listed securities and deposits the required 50 percent ($5,000) into the account.

Market value	$10,000
Debit balance	5,000
Equity	5,000

If the market value declines to $8,000, how does the customer's account stand in regard to the NYSE minimum maintenance requirement? The procedure for determining this is similar to that of recomputing the account for buying power. The only difference is the requirement of 25 percent as opposed to 50 percent.

Market value	$8,000
Debit balance	5,000
Equity	3,000

At this point, calculate 25 percent of the current market value:

$$25\% \times \$8,000 = \$2,000$$

Req.	Eq.	
$2,000	$3,000	
	2,000	
	$1,000	excess over NYSE
		maintenance requirement

As you can see, the requirement is $2,000 versus an equity of $3,000, leaving an excess of $1,000. This excess cannot be withdrawn or converted into buying power, because it is only excess over the NYSE minimum maintenance requirement. This means that this account could withstand even further market decline without incurring a maintenance call.

Suppose the market value declines further to $6,000. How would the account stand?

Market value	$6,000
Debit balance	5,000
Equity	1,000

Maintenance Requirement = 25% × $6,000 = $1,500

Req.	Eq.
$1,500	$1,000

We now have a situation where the requirement exceeds the customer's equity. If you subtract the equity from the requirement, this will tell you how much the customer must deposit to bring the account back into compliance with the NYSE maintenance requirement.

	Req.	Eq.
	$1,500	$1,000
	−1,000	
NYSE maintenance call	500	

This customer would be contacted to deposit at least $500.

Just like a Federal call, a NYSE maintenance call may be answered in any of four ways:

1. The customer can deposit the required funds.
2. The customer can liquidate stocks (sell securities).
3. The customer can deposit additional securities.
4. The market can appreciate.

Should the customer answer the maintenance call by depositing money, the effect on the account would be as follows:

Market value	$6,000
Debit balance	4,500
Equity	1,500

The deposit of the money will reduce the debit balance and increase the equity by $500. Remember, anytime money is deposited into the margin account the debit balance is reduced and the equity is increased by the amount of the deposit, regardless of the reason for the deposit.

Req.	**Eq.**
$1,500	$1,500

The account is now in compliance with NYSE rules. As this account is right on the line, most brokers would ask for more than the $500 required.

In the event the customer does not want to deposit the additional funds but wishes to sell securities, simply multiply the amount of the maintenance call by four:

Market value	$6,000
Debit balance	5,000
Equity	1,000

	Req.	**Eq.**
	$1,500	$1,000
	−1,000	
NYSE maintenance call	500	

The NYSE call is $500. $500 × 4 = $2,000. This customer must sell $2,000 in securities to bring the account back into compliance with NYSE rules.

After the sale, the account would appear thus:

Market value	$4,000
Debit balance	3,000
Equity	1,000

The sale of $2,000 reduces the market value and the debit balance by $2,000. Recompute the account and see how the account stands from the

NYSE maintenance requirements. In this case, find 25 percent of the new current market value: 25% × $4,000 = $1,000.

Req.	Eq.
$1,000	$1,000

The account is back in compliance with the NYSE maintenance requirements.

Another way of meeting the NYSE call is by depositing additional collateral using the same account:

Market value	$6,000
Debit balance	5,000
Equity	1,000

Once again, the account is on NYSE call for $500.

Let's say the customer wanted to meet the call by bringing in additional collateral. What is the minimum market value of securities that must be deposited? To determine the amount, simply multiply NYSE call amount by 4/3. On the account above:

$$\frac{4}{3} \times \$500 = \frac{\$2,000}{3} = \$666$$

The customer would have to deposit securities with a market value of $666.

Why couldn't the customer bring in just $500 worth of securities? Once the additional collateral is received into the account, those securities become subject to the NYSE 25 percent maintenance requirement. Consequently, the additional collateral is needed to bring the entire account up to 25 percent. After the deposit of the additional collateral, the account would now appear as follows:

Market value	$6,666
Debit balance	5,000
Equity	1,666

The deposit of the additional collateral will increase the market value and the customer's equity. However, this additional collateral in no way affects the customer's debit balance. If you recomputed the account now, you will see that the account meets the NYSE minimum maintenance requirements:

$$25\% \times \$6,666 = \$1,666$$

The last way of meeting an NYSE maintenance call would be through market appreciation. This would happen if the market value increased in a relatively short period of time to the point where the account would meet the NYSE minimum requirements. We can determine the price the securities would have to rise to by simply multiplying 4/3 the debit balance:

$$4/3 \times \$5,000 = \$6,666$$

Therefore, should the market value of the securities in the account increase to $6,666, the account would meet the NYSE minimum maintenance requirements. Allowing for the meeting of the call by market appreciation is at the discretion of the broker. Many brokers will not allow it. The reasoning is that market fluctuations will cause the customer to be on call one day, off the next. It becomes difficult to keep track of the fluctuations, and the chance for error and violation of the rules multiplies.

Thus far, when looking at the NYSE minimum maintenance requirements, we have looked only at the customer's margin account. Suppose the customer also has a cash account and has securities in it. The securities held in the customer's cash account may also be used to supply the necessary margin. The safest way to make this happen is to transfer the securities from the cash account to the margin account. However, the customer may not want to do this. In fact, the securities may not be eligible for the margin account. Many over-the-counter (OTC) securities are not permitted in the customer's margin account, nor do they have loan value.

However, these securities have value from the standpoint that they can be sold. Using our account, assume the customer also has a cash account with $6,000 market value of non-marginable over-the-counter securities.

Margin Account		**Cash Account**	
Market value	$6,000	Market value	$6,000
Debit balance	5,000		
Equity	1,000		

Recompute for NYSE minimum maintenance requirements:

Req.	**Eq.**
$1,500	$1,000
1,500	6,000
3,000	$7,000

In this example, we used 25 percent of the current market value in the margin account ($6,000 \times 25\% = \$1,500$) and its equity of $1,000. Now look at the cash account. To use the customer's cash account to support his margin account, the equity in the cash account must be compared to the same margin requirements as those in the margin account. This is why there is an additional $1,500 under the requirement side (25% × $6,000 = $1,500). Note that the full market value of $6,000 is used on the equity side. Since there is never a debit balance in the cash account, the equity is the same amount as the market value. Therefore, the customer has a total requirement of $3,000 versus a total equity of $7,000. There is now an excess in the combined accounts, so there would be no NYSE minimum maintenance call. Keep in mind that while we are looking to the cash account to support the margin account, the securities must remain in the cash account.

One variation is known as a *guaranteed account*. This is a situation where one account supports another, but the accounts belong to different individuals. For instance, a husband might guarantee his wife's account or vice versa; or a father might guarantee his child's account. If such a situation exists, the guarantee must be in writing and should state the dollar amount of the limit of the guarantee.

J. Jones		**W. Smith**	
Margin Account		**Margin Account**	
Market value	$40,000	Market value	$6,000
Debit balance	17,000	Debit balance	5,000
Equity	23,000	Equity	1,000

Req.	Eq.	
$1,500	$1,000	Smith Account
10,000	23,000	Jones Account
$11,500	$24,000	Combined

The above accounts were simply combined to see how they stand on a combined basis. Mr. Smith's account is undermargined, but when combined with Mr. Jones's account, both would satisfy the NYSE requirements.

A word of caution: Guarantees should be checked on a regular basis to ensure they are still in effect. Should Mr. Jones cancel his guarantee, Mr. Smith would have a call for $500.

How much time does a customer have to meet a maintenance call? Rule 431 of the NYSE sets the maximum time limit as 15 business days from the date the account went below the NYSE limits. Fifteen business days is a very long time, and most firms would not go along with that amount of time. However, maintenance calls are different than T calls in this regard. A customer who purchases securities knows he must pay for them within a specified period of time. The customer makes his commitment at the time he purchases securities.

A maintenance call is occasioned by market activity. This may be a long-standing customer who has just had the market go against him or her. Under these circumstances, a firm may want to extend the time for the client to the time limit permissible.

CHAPTER THREE QUESTIONS

1. A maintenance call is:

    a. a request for funds as a result of a purchase.
    b. that amount required when the margin account is initially opened.
    c. also called a Regulation T call.
    d. a request for funds when market changes decrease an account's equity below the broker's maintenance requirements.

2. The New York Stock Exchange's minimum maintenance requirement for long positions is:

    a. 25 percent of the market value.
    b. 50 percent of the market value.
    c. 25 percent of the equity in a customer's account.
    d. 50 percent of the debit balance.

3. Excess over minimum maintenance is:

    a. the amount by which the loan value exceeds the maintenance requirements.
    b. the amount by which the loan value exceeds the debit balance.
    c. the amount by which the account's equity exceeds the maintenance requirement.
    d. the amount over the Regulation T requirement.

4. Excess over NYSE minimum maintenance may:

    a. be withdrawn.
    b. be used to purchase additional securities.
    c. not be withdrawn.
    d. none of the above.

5. A customer opens a margin account with an initial transaction of a purchase of 100 ABC at 24. Regulation T requirements are 50 percent. How much must the customer deposit?

    a. $1,200
    b. $2,400
    c. $1,000
    d. $2,000

6. A customer's margin account is as follows:

Market value	$18,000
Debit balance	13,900
Equity	4,100

This account is under NYSE minimum maintenance requirements by:

a. $4,900.
b. $400.
c. $2,000.
d. $500.

7. (Same account as in Question 6.) The customer wishes to meet the call by liquidation. How much must the customer sell?

a. $1,600
b. $4,900
c. $2,000
d. $13,900

8. (Same account as in Question 6.) The equity in the customer's account after the liquidation would:

a. increase by 50 percent of the proceeds.
b. decrease.
c. increase by the amount of the sale.
d. not change.

9. A customer's margin account is as follows:

Market value	$23,000
Debit balance	18,000
Equity	5,000

The account is on NYSE maintenance call for $750. The customer wishes to deposit marginable securities into the account. What is the minimum amount required?

a. $1,000
b. $1,600
c. $3,200
d. $800

10. (Same account as in Question 9.) How long may the broker wait to receive the required funds?

a. seven business days
b. five business days
c. fifteen business days
d. promptly

CHAPTER 4

The Special Memorandum Account

The special memorandum account, more commonly referred to as the SMA, is unquestionably the most misunderstood account on Wall Street. Although the SMA is a separate account as defined by Section 220.5 of Regulation T, it works hand in hand with the customer's margin account. This section of Regulation T defines the account and the permissible entries, the wording of which may explain why it is so misunderstood:

1. A special memorandum account (SMA) may be maintained in conjunction with a margin account. A single entry amount may be used to represent both a credit to the SMA and a debit to the margin account. A transfer between the two accounts may be affected by an increase or reduction in the entry. When computing the equity in a margin account, the single entry shall be considered as a debit in the margin account. A payment to the customer or on the customer's behalf or a transfer to any of the customer's other accounts from the SMA reduces the single entry amount.

2. The SMA may contain the following entries:
   a. dividend and interest payments;
   b. cash not required by this part, including cash deposited to meet a maintenance margin call or to meet any requirement of a self-regulatory organization that is not imposed by this part;
   c. proceeds of a sale of securities or cash no longer required on any expired or liquidated security position that may be withdrawn under section 220.4(e) of this part; and

d. margin excess transferred from the margin account under section 220.4(e)(2) of this part.

The primary purpose of the SMA is to preserve the customer's buying power. As we discussed earlier, buying power is created by having equity in excess of the Regulation T requirement. Here is an example:

Market value	$10,000
Debit balance	4,000
Equity	6,000

Req.	**Eq.**	
$5,000	$6,000	
	−5,000	
	1,000	excess
	x 2	
	$2,000	buying power

As you can see, this customer has excess equity of $1,000, which may be withdrawn or converted into buying power of $2,000 (the customer can purchase $2,000 of securities without depositing any additional funds). However, if the customer did not withdraw the excess funds or purchase additional securities, and the market value of the securities declined to $9,000, the account would look like this:

Market value	$9,000
Debit balance	4,000
Equity	5,000

Req.	**Eq.**	
$4,500	$5,000	
	−4,500	
	500	excess
	x 2	
	$1,000	buying power

By not acting immediately, this customer lost $500 of excess equity, thereby reducing buying power to $1,000. When refiguring a margin account, remember to use the current market value versus the current requirement.

Up until the 1930s, the procedure for preventing a customer from losing buying power was to take the excess out of the customer's margin account and put it into the customer's cash account. This was accomplished by debiting the customer's margin account and crediting the customer's cash account via a journal entry. In addition, an account receivable and an account payable had to be established in the accounting department to reflect the offsetting debit and credit entries. Further complicating this was the adjustment of the customer's debit balance at the end of each month to ensure that the proper interest was charged. This was all done manually and was quite labor intensive.

In the early 1940s, a bright young margin clerk by the name of Aaron Schwaberg read Regulation T and saw a section where a *special miscellaneous account* could be established to meet the needs of the customer. The account was renamed the special memorandum account in 1983 to better describe the entries and actual use of the account. In any event, the account has long since been referred to as the SMA.

This clerk simply took the customer's margin card (which reflected the customer's holdings, total market value, debit balance and equity) and drew the following on the back of the card (the beginning of the special memorandum account):[1]

SMA
DATE DEBIT CREDIT BALANCE EXPLANATION

This account preserved the customer's buying power, and since it was a memorandum method of accounting, it eliminated a whole bookkeeping record in the accounting department and the accompanying journal entries.

An example of the memorandum method follows:

Customer's Margin Account

Market value	$10,000
Debit balance	4,000
Equity	6,000

Req.	Eq.
$5,000	$6,000
	−5,000
	1,000
	excess

The $1,000 is placed in the SMA:

DATE	DEBIT	CREDIT	BALANCE	EXPLANATION
12/11/07		$1,000	$1,000	Excess over Reg. T

---

[1] Appendix B shows the actual hand posted sheets of the customer margin and SMA accounts.

The $1,000 excess is now in a special memorandum account that is a separate and distinct account preserving the customer's buying power of $2,000.

The customer's margin account would still appear the same.

There is no increase in the customer's debit balance because the entry to the SMA is a memorandum entry—monies have not left the firm and there has been no additional extension of credit. Consequently, there is no increase in the customer's debit balance.

If the market value of the customer's securities declines to $9,000, the customer would still have buying power of $2,000, since the $1,000 excess was moved to the SMA. In fact, this customer could still withdraw the $1,000. Withdrawals from the SMA are always permitted as long as they do not put the account below the NYSE minimum maintenance margin requirements. The margin account now looks like this:

Market value	$9,000
Debit balance	4,000
Equity	5,000

Should the customer withdraw the money from the SMA, the SMA would look like this:

Date	Debit	Credit	Balance	Explanation
12/11/07		$1,000	$1,000	Excess over Reg. T
12/12/07	$1,000		0	Withdrawal

The customer's margin account would now appear as follows:

Market value	$9,000
Debit balance	5,000
Equity	4,000

Notice that the debit balance is now increased by the actual withdrawal because the funds have, in fact, left the firm, and there was an additional extension of credit. In the event the customer purchased $2,000 of securities instead of withdrawing the funds, the margin account would appear as follows:

Market value	$11,000
Debit balance	7,000
Equity	4,000

The proper entry to the SMA would be as follows:

Date	Debit	Credit	Balance	Explanation
12/11/07		$1,000	$1,000	Excess over Reg. T
12/12/07	$1,000		0	Pur. 100 ABC at 20

The SMA is the official record of the customer's account. All entries are permanent and require descriptions informative enough to detail what took place.

Here is a sample of a customer's account, giving the proper entries to the customer's margin and SMA accounts, along with detailed explanations.

CUSTOMER'S ACCOUNT

(Assume that the following positions are all long and were purchased sometime in the past, and the required margin was deposited.)

Margin Account of John Smith (Long)

100	A	24	$2,400
200	B	13	$2,600
100	C	10	$1,000
200	D	24	$4,800

Market value	$10,800
Debit balance	3,200
Equity	7,600

Req.	**Eq.**
$4,500	$7,600
	−5,400
	2,200

excess over Reg. T

The entry to the SMA would be as follows:

Date	Debit	Credit	Balance	Explanation
1/4/08		$2,200	$2,200	Excess over Reg. T

All we have done at this point is determined the customer's total market value and then recomputed the account to see if there was any excess over the current Regulation T margin requirement of 50 percent. There was, in the amount of $2,200.

The customer now withdraws $1,000.

Date	Debit	Credit	Balance	Explanation
1/4/08		$2,200	$2,200	Excess over Reg. T
1/7/08	$1,000		1,200	Withdrawal

Customer's Margin Account

Market value	$10,800
Debit balance	4,200
Equity	6,600

The customer's debit balance was increased and equity was decreased to reflect the withdrawal of $1,000.

Now the customer purchases 100 shares of E at 50.

Margin Account

100	A	24	$2,400
200	B	13	$2,600
100	C	10	$1,000
200	D	24	$4,800
100	E	50	$5,000

Market value	$15,800
Debit balance	9,200
Equity	6,600

As a result of the purchase of 100 E at 50 the market value is increased by $5,000, as well as the debit balance. The purchase of 100 E at 50 ($5,000) requires 50 percent or $2,500 under Reg. T. If we look to the customer's SMA, a portion of the money is there.

Date	Debit	Credit	Balance	Explanation
1/4/08		$2,200	$2,200	Excess over Reg. T
1/7/08	$1,000		1,200	Withdrawal
1/8/08	1,200		0	Buy 100 E at 50, T call $1,300

There was a requirement for $2,500, and $1,200 was available in the customer's SMA. The $1,200 was subtracted from the balance in the SMA (applied to the T call), and $1,200 was subtracted from the requirement (supplied from the SMA). A Regulation T call was issued for $1,300. Note that the *Balance* column in the SMA can only be a credit balance or a zero balance—never a debit balance.

The customer now deposits the required $1,300. The account would appear as follows:

Market value	$15,800
Debit balance	7,900
Equity	7,900

The debit balance is reduced by the amount of the deposit. However, there is no entry to the customer's SMA. This is because the money deposited was used to meet the Regulation T call. Any time money is deposited, it will always reduce the debit balance. In addition, the deposit will be a credit to the SMA, provided it is not needed to meet a Fed or Reg. T call.

Dividends of $1.00 per share are declared on the holdings of 100 A, 200 B, and 100 C.

Market value	$15,800
Debit balance	7,500
Equity	8,300

The money received ($400) would reduce the customer's debit balance. Again, any time money is received into the account, the debit balance is reduced. Now, since the monies received were not required by Regulation T, they may be placed into the customer's SMA.

Date	Debit	Credit	Balance	Explanation
1/4/08		$2,200	$2,200	Excess over Reg. T
1/7/08	$1,000		1,200	Withdrawal
1/8/08	1,200		0	Buy 100 E at 50, T call $1,300
1/9/08		400	400	Div. $1.00 on 100 A, 200 B 100 C

Now let's assume the market value of the securities declines as follows:

100	A	20	$2,000
200	B	10	$2,000
100	C	6	$600
200	D	19	$3,800
100	E	37	$3,700

Market value	$12,100
Debit balance	7,500
Equity	4,600

Any time there is a sharp decline in the market value of securities, the margin account should be checked to see how the account stands as far as meeting the NYSE minimum maintenance requirement of 25 percent.

Req.	Eq.	
$3,025	$4,600	
	−3,025	
	1,575	excess over NYSE min. maint. Req.

What if the customer wishes to withdraw $200? This is a permissible withdrawal because the customer's margin account would still be above NYSE maintenance after the withdrawal.

The margin account after the withdrawal looks like this:

Market value	$12,100
Debit balance	7,700
Equity	4,400

The entry to the SMA would then be as follows:

Date	Debit	Credit	Balance	Explanation
1/4/08		$2,200	$2,200	Excess over Reg. T
1/7/08	$1,000		$1,200	Withdrawal
1/8/08	$1,200		0	Buy 100 E at 50, T call $1,300
1/9/08		400	400	Div. $1.00 on 100 A, 200 B, 100 C
1/10/08	200		200	

The customer sells 200 B at 10. After the sale of securities the account will appear as follows:

100	A	20	$2,000
100	C	6	$600
200	D	19	$3,800
100	E	37	$3,700

Market value	$10,100
Debit balance	5,700
Equity	4,400

Sales of securities will release funds in the amount of 50 percent of the sale proceeds.

The entry to the SMA looks like this:

Date	Debit	Credit	Balance	Explanation
1/4/08		$2,200	$2,200	Excess over Reg. T
1/7/08	$1,000		$1,200	Withdrawal
1/8/08	$1,200		0	Buy 100 E at 50, T call $1,300
1/9/08		400	400	Div. $1.00 on 100 A, 200 B, 100 C
1/10/08	200		200	Withdrawal
1/11/08		$1,000	$1,200	Sale of 200 B at 10

The customer now withdraws $1,200 cash. The entry to the SMA looks like this: .

Date	Debit	Credit	Balance	Explanation
1/4/08		$2,200	$2,200	Excess over Reg. T
1/7/08	$1,000		$1,200	Withdrawal
1/8/08	$1,200		0	Buy 100 E at 50, T call $1,300
1/9/08		400	400	Div. $1.00 on 100 A, 200 B, 100 C
1/10/08	200		200	Withdrawal
1/11/08		$1,000	$1,200	Sale of 200 B at 10
1/14/08	1,200		0	Withdrawal

After the withdrawal, the customer's margin account is as follows:

Market value	$10,100
Debit balance	6,900
Equity	3,200

Customer sells 100 A at 20:

100	C	6	$600
200	D	19	$3,800
100	E	37	$3,700

Market value	$8,100
Debit balance	4,900
Equity	3,200

Now the entry to the SMA looks like this:

Date	Debit	Credit	Balance	Explanation
1/4/08		$2,200	$2,200	Excess over Reg. T
1/7/08	$1,000		$1,200	Withdrawal
1/8/08	$1,200		0	Buy 100 E at 50, T call $1,300
1/9/08		400	400	Div. $1.00 on 100 A, 200 B, 100 C
1/10/08	200		200	Withdrawal
1/11/08		$1,000	$1,200	Sale of 200 B at 10
1/14/08	1,200		0	Withdrawal
1/15/08		$1000	$1,000	Sale of 100 A at 20

What happens if the market value of D drops to 9 per share?

100	C	6	$600
200	D	9	$1,800
100	E	37	$3,700

Market value	$6,100
Debit balance	4,900
Equity	1,200

In light of the market decline, let us examine how this affects the account from the standpoint of NYSE minimum maintenance requirements.

	Req.	**Eq.**
	$1,525	$1,200
	−1,200	
NYSE call	$ 325	

This account is on stock exchange maintenance margin call for $325. In our example, we will request the $325, and assume that *the customer deposits the requested amount*. The customer's margin account will reflect this as follows:

Market value	$6,100
Debit balance	4,575
Equity	1,525

Money came into the account, thereby reducing the debit balance by the amount of the deposit ($325). Additionally, since the funds were not required by Regulation T, they may be credited to the customer's SMA by the amount of the deposit. The customer's SMA reflects this:

Date	**Debit**	**Credit**	**Balance**	**Explanation**
1/4/08		$2,200	$2,200	Excess over Reg. T
1/7/08	$1,000		$1,200	Withdrawal
1/8/08	$1,200		0	Buy 100 E at 50, T call $1,300
1/9/08		400	400	Div. $1.00 on 100 A, 200 B, 100 C
1/10/08	200		200	Withdrawal
1/11/08		$1,000	$1,200	Sale of 200 B at 10
1/14/08	1,200		0	Withdrawal
1/15/08		$1000	$1,000	Sale of 100 A at 20
1/16/08		$325	$1,325	Deposit of funds to meet NYSE call

As you can see, the balance in the customer's SMA is $1,325; however, the customer may not withdraw any of these funds, as a withdrawal would put the account below NYSE minimum maintenance requirements. At the same time, the balance would not be eliminated, for if the market rises, the customer could use part or all of these funds, depending on the increase in the account's market value.

Market value of the securities increase is as follows:

100	C	25	$2,500
200	D	15	$3,000
100	E	40	$4,000

Market value	$9,500
Debit balance	4,575
Equity	4,925

There appears to be excess over Regulation T; therefore, the account should be recomputed:

Req.	Eq.	
$4,750	$4,925	
	−4,750	
	175	excess over Reg. T

The $175 excess over Regulation T may not be credited to the SMA because the excess is less than the current balance of the SMA ($175 excess over Reg. T versus $1,325 balance in SMA). However, in the event Reg. T excess exceeds the current balance in the SMA, the difference may be made up in the SMA. For example, if the excess over Regulation T came to $1,600, $275 could be credited to the SMA to bring it from $1,325 to $1,600. In our example, this is not the case, so no entry is made to the SMA.

The customer purchases 100 F at 50:

100	C	25	$2,500
200	D	15	$3,000
100	E	40	$4,000
100	F	50	$5,000

Market value	$14,500
Debit balance	9,575
Equity	4,925

The $5,000 purchase requires 50 percent, or $2,500. The customer's SMA has $1,325.

Required	$2,500
SMA	1,325
Reg. T call	1,175

Date	Debit	Credit	Balance	Explanation
1/4/08		$2,200	$2,200	Excess over Reg. T
1/7/08	$1,000		$1,200	Withdrawal
1/8/08	$1,200		0	Buy 100 E at 50, T call $1,300
1/9/08		400	400	Div. $1.00 on 100 A, 200 B, 100 C
1/10/08	200		200	Withdrawal
1/11/08		$1,000	$1,200	Sale of 200 B at 10
1/14/08	1,200		0	Withdrawal
1/15/08		$1000	$1,000	Sale of 100 A at 20
1/16/08		$325	$1,325	Deposit of funds to meet NYSE call
1/17/08	1,325		0	Buy 100 F at 50 T call $1,175

After the deposit of funds to meet the Regulation T call, the account now appears as follows:

Market value	$14,500
Debit balance	8,400
Equity	6,100

No entry to the customer's SMA is made because the funds deposited were required by Regulation T. Only the customer's debit balance was reduced. Also note that the customer's margin account is still classified as restricted, just as it was for a good portion of the month. Yet this in no way restricted the customer's ability to trade.

CHAPTER FOUR QUESTIONS

1. The SMA is used to:
   a. satisfy NYSE calls.
   b. satisfy house calls.
   c. purchase securities.
   d. preserve the customer's buying power.

2. A withdrawal of funds from the SMA will always:
   a. increase the customer's debit balance.
   b. increase the customer's equity.
   c. be permitted.
   d. increase the market value of securities held in the customer's margin account.

3. Cash deposited to meet an outstanding Regulation T call will:
   a. increase the debit balance.
   b. not affect the SMA.
   c. decrease the equity in the account.
   d. increase the market value of securities.

4. If fully paid-for listed securities are deposited in a customer's margin account, the customer may credit the customer's SMA:
   a. zero.
   b. 100 percent of the current market value of the securities.
   c. 50 percent of the current market value of the securities.
   d. 25 percent of the current market value of the securities.

5. Monies in the SMA may be withdrawn:
   a. only if after the withdrawal the margin account would not be restricted.
   b. to purchase securities only.
   c. in amounts of $2,000 or more.
   d. provided the account was above minimum maintenance requirements after withdrawal.

6. As a result of increasing interest rates, a customer reduced his debit balance by depositing $10,000 into his margin account. The proper entry to the SMA would be:
   a. credit the SMA $10,000.
   b. to reduce his debit balance.
   c. no entry to the SMA.
   d. none of the above.

7. A customer is on NYSE maintenance call for $750. The customer sends a check for $750. The proper entry to the SMA would be:
   a. no entry to the SMA.
   b. credit the account $750.
   c. credit the account $1,500.
   d. debit the account $750.

8. A customer's margin account is on NYSE maintenance call for $1,000. The customer also has a balance of $5,000 in her SMA and instructs her

broker to take the $1,000 out of her SMA to meet the maintenance call. The proper entry to the SMA would be:

    a. debit the account $1,000.

    b. credit the account $1,000.

    c. no entry to the SMA; improper request.

    d. credit margin account, debit SMA.

  9. Dividend received on a holding in the margin account may:

    a. be credited to the SMA.

    b. be debited to the SMA.

    c. increase the debit balance.

    d. decrease the customer's equity.

10. A customer's margin account has excess over Regulation T of $1,500 and a credit balance of $1,700 in his SMA. What would you be permitted to do?

    a. increase SMA by $200

    b. decrease SMA by $200

    c. credit SMA 50 percent of $1,500

    d. nothing

Short Sales

Prior to describing the actual mechanics of short selling, a little background information may be helpful. Up to this point, we have been describing purchases on margin that create a *long* position. If you own securities, you are considered long. When you sell these securities, it is a *long sale*.

As you know, the vast majority of investors look for a corporation that has a good product or product line, look into the management (Is it efficient? innovative? aggressive?), check the competition, and look at the price of the security. If they believe the security is undervalued, investors will buy with the expectation that the price will increase, resulting in a profit.

The short seller investigates in the same way but is looking for an outdated product, poor management, and strong competition. This investor feels the security is overvalued. Consequently, this investor will sell the security with the intention of buying it back some time in the future at a cheaper price, again resulting in a profit.

A short sale is defined by the Securities Exchange Act of 1934 as the sale of a security not owned by the investor, or if owned, the investor does not intend to deliver. In most business transactions, if you sell something you don't own, you probably will go to jail for fraud. In the securities industry it is done all the time. Fraud is avoided by borrowing securities and delivering the borrowed securities to the buyer.

To have any transaction, there must be a buyer and a seller; the same applies with short sales. However, this transaction differs slightly in that a third party is involved, a *lender*.

The lender is usually an institution or broker-dealer but may be an individual who has a large, well-diversified portfolio and is willing to lend the securities.

One of the requirements to sell short is that you must be in a position to borrow the securities. The short seller borrows the securities and, in turn, sells them to the buyer. When he delivers the securities to the buyer he receives payment.

At this point one wonders, "Why would the owner of the securities lend them to the short seller in the first place?" The lender is going to receive as collateral 100 percent of the market value (or the proceeds) of the short sale.

This is what makes the stock loan business so profitable. Remember, the lender is still the owner of the security. The lender did not sell or give it to the short seller—he lent it. As the owner of the security, the lender is entitled to all dividends and distributions such as rights offerings and spin-offs and also market appreciation.

As a result of this short sale, we have created two 100 ABC long positions; one is the buyer, the other the lender. Therefore, any distribution by the company must be met by the short seller to the lender. If a $100 dividend is declared, when it is payable, the short seller pays the lender. If a rights offering is made, the short seller must purchase the rights in the open market and deliver the rights to the lender. If there is a stock split, the short seller now owes the lender 200 shares. As you see, the lender is still very much the owner of the security. The only privilege that the lender may lose is the right to vote (a small consideration compared to the benefits).

The lender has converted the portfolio from stock certificates to cash and still retains ownership. As a result of having this excess cash, the lender will invest it in some money market instrument such as a Treasury bill, certificates of deposit, bankers' acceptance, or commercial paper. Therefore, the lender's net worth is enhanced by whatever interest is earned on the money market instruments. In addition, the lender is completely protected. The lender has 100 percent of the market value, and, should the short seller disappear, the lender has sufficient money to repurchase the stock and go back to the original position.

In order to protect the lender as well as the short seller, the brokerage firm goes through a procedure known as *mark to the market* to ensure that the lender will have 100 percent of the current market value of the securities regardless of market fluctuations. Our example looks like this:

Short Seller	**Lender**
−100 ABC	+$10,000

If the market value of 100 ABC increased to $12,000, the lender would no longer have 100 percent of the market value of the securities. So the brokerage firm would take $2,000 from the short seller's account and give it to the lender to boost the collateral to its proper level. This is accomplished by debiting the short seller $2,000 and crediting the lender $2,000. After the mark to the market is complete, our example now looks this way:

Short Seller	**Lender**
−100 ABC	+$12,000
$2,000 debit	

Now suppose the reverse happens and the market value declines to $9,000. The lender is holding $12,000, and the securities borrowed are worth only $9,000. The lender has too much. Therefore, a *reverse mark to the market* is made, crediting the short seller's account and debiting the lender's account. Again, the lender is entitled to only 100 percent of the market value. Our example now looks like this:

Short Seller	**Lender**
−100 ABC	+$9,000
$1,000 credit	

As a result of crediting the short seller with $3,000, the $2,000 debit balance was eliminated and, in fact, a credit balance was created. The lender's credit was reduced to $9,000.

To close out his position, the short seller must return 100 ABC to the lender. He might buy the shares in the open market for $9,000 and return them. Once the 100 ABC is returned, the lender must return the collateral—in this case, $9,000. In fact, the $9,000 collateral that the lender surrenders is used to pay for the purchase of the 100 ABC.

Short Seller	**Lender**
$1,000 credit	100 ABC
Seller of the 100 ABC	
$9,000	

The short seller has repaid the stock loan, the lender has the 100 ABC, the seller of the securities has been paid, and there is a $1,000 credit balance in the short seller's account, representing his profit. In the event the short seller closed the position at $12,000, a $2,000 debit would exist in the account representing the short seller's loss.

There are several additional important points regarding short sales. As previously stated, a prerequisite to selling short is the ability to borrow the securities. Most firms have a department called the *stock loan department* that arranges for the loans either within or outside the firm.

When a short sale is entered into, the order must be marked as *short*. All sell orders are identified as long (you are the owner) or short (you are selling borrowed securities).

Thus far, we have examined the mechanics of the short sale. What does this look like in the customer's margin account? Years ago, when posting was done manually, margin clerks always separated long positions from short positions by keeping all of the long positions on one side of the card and all short positions on the other, making it easy to distinguish one from the other.

Along came the computer and made it necessary to separate long and short positions by placing them in separate records. Thus, you hear the term *short account*. Though it may sound like a different account, the short account is simply a part of the customer's margin account.

In fact, Regulation T requires all short sales to be made in the margin account. Using the same short sale transaction described previously, we will see how this transaction is handled in the customer's margin account.

Let's look at a scenario where the customer sells short 100 ABC for $10,000.

Customer's Margin Account
Short Account
$10,000, SMV
$10,000 credit

The short sale is placed in the customer's short account. This triggers a T-call for $5,000. As in purchases, the customer is required to deposit 50 percent of the short market value in accordance with Regulation T. The same time restrictions apply (deposit promptly—three business days, must be received in five business days). Assume the customer deposits the required amount ($5,000). Our customer's margin account after the deposit appears as follows:

Margin Account	**Short Account**
$5,000 credit	$10,000 SMV
	10,000 credit

Notice that the $5,000 credit was placed in the customer's margin account and not in the short account. If the customer had a debit balance, the debit would have to be reduced by the amount of the deposit. The SMV (short market value) is $10,000. However, the credit balance under the SMV is known as a *ledger credit balance*. That credit balance represents the proceeds of the short sale that are not in the customer's account but are securing the stock loan, enabling the customer to make the short sale and then deliver the borrowed shares.

As the market value increases to $12,000, here is what the account would look like:

Margin Account	**Short Account**
$5,000 credit	$12,000 SMV
	10,000 credit

Looking at the credit in the short account, it is clear that the lender does not have the full market value of the shares being lent. Now we must mark the transaction to the market. We would take $2,000 from the short seller and send it to the lender. Afterward, the account would look like this:

Margin Account	**Short Account**
$3,000 credit	$12,000 SMV
	12,000 credit

You can see that the lender now has 100 percent of the market value, and the credit in the customer's margin account was reduced by the amount of the mark to the market.

Next, we indicated that the market value declined to $9,000 (the short seller was correct—the market value of the securities went down). The short seller's account would now appear as follows:

Margin Account	**Short Account**
$3,000 credit	$9,000 SMV
	12,000 credit

Again, it is clear the market value of the sold securities is now $9,000, but the lender is holding $12,000 as collateral. Now we will perform a reverse mark to the market. The lender will send the short seller $3,000 and our account would look like this:

Margin Account	**Short Account**
$6,000 credit	$9,000 SMV
	9,000 credit

This account as it stands, has $1,500 excess over Regulation T and $3,000 *buying power.*

Req.	Eq.	
$4,500	$6,000	
	−4,500	
	1,500	excess
	× 2	
	$3,000	buying power or short selling power

The same principle of recomputing the Regulation T requirement applies to the account on the short side as on the long side: The 50 percent requirement of the current market value, whether it is long market value or short market value is used to determine the Reg. T excess.

The equity in this short account is calculated by subtracting the short market value from the credit balance ($9,000 − $9,000 = 0). However, long and short accounts *must be combined* when recomputing the margin account. In our example there is no long market value and no debit balance in the margin account, just a credit balance of $6,000. This is the equity.

The excess of $1,500 may also be placed in the customer's SMA for future use. Let's assume that the customer wishes to buy $3,000 of listed securities in the margin account. After the purchase, the account would appear as follows:

Margin Account   **Short Account**
MV $3,000   SMV $9,000
Credit 3,000   Credit 9,000
Equity 6,000

Notice that the credit balance in the long account decreased by the full amount of the purchase, yet the equity remained the same. All we did was change the composition of the equity. Instead of all cash, the equity is now a mixture of cash and securities. Recomputation of the account now will show the account is right at the 50 percent level.

Req.	Eq.
$1,500	$6,000
4,500	0
$6,000	6,000

Fifty percent of the long market value is $1,500; equity in the account is $6,000; 50 percent of the short market value is $4,500; and equity on the short side is zero. Equity on the short side will always be zero, because the short market value and the credit balance are marked to the market on a daily basis.

COVERING SHORT SALES

The term *covering a short sale* simply means a customer closes out the short position by purchasing the securities that were sold short and returning them to the lender. (Short sales may also be covered by delivering a long position to the lender. This procedure will be discussed later.)
Here is our account now:

Margin Account				Short Account			
100	A	at 10	$1,000	100	X	at 40	$4,000
100	B	at 12	1,200	100	Y	at 50	5,000
100	C	at 8	800				
Market value			$3,000	Short market value			$9,000
Credit balance			3,000	Credit balance			9,000
Equity			6,000				

The customer wishes to close out the short position of 100 Y at 50. The customer would enter a buy order for 100 Y. When purchased, it will be delivered to the lender to repay the stock borrowed. The effect on the customer's account is as follows:

Margin Account				Short Account			
100	A	at 10	$1,000	100	X	at 40	$4,000
100	B	at 12	1,200				
100	C	at 8	800				
Market value			$3,000	Short market value			$4,000
Credit balance			3,000	Credit balance			4,000
Equity			6,000				

The SMA would look like this:

Date	Debit	Credit	Balance	Explanation
1/7/08		$2,500		Pur. 100 Y to cover short

Covering a short position reduces the short market value as well as the credit balance. The credit balance is reduced because we have returned the stock to the lender. Consequently, the lender had to return the collateral ($5,000). In fact, we used that $5,000 to purchase the 100 Y. The credit to the customer's SMA represents the permissible release on the covering of a short sale, 50 percent of the cost. Hence, cost of cover was $5,000, and 50 percent of this is $2,500—the amount credited to the SMA.

To summarize briefly, short sales of securities are subject to Regulation T just as are long purchases: 50 percent of short sale proceeds must be deposited into the customer's account "promptly"—no later than five business days.

NYSE MINIMUM MAINTENANCE REQUIREMENTS

Just as on the long side, the short side has minimum maintenance requirements as well. However, they are a little more complex. As previously stated, a short sale is a risky position, as one could suffer unlimited losses. Consequently, the NYSE established higher requirements on low-priced securities. This is because the chance of a security that is selling at $60 or $70 per share doubling in a short period of time is relatively small compared to the chance of a security selling at $2 or $3 doing so. Therefore, Rule 431 of the NYSE requires the following minimum maintenance for short sales:

- $2.50 per share or 100 percent of the market value, whichever amount is greater for each stock selling below $5.00 per share.
- $5.00 per share or 30 percent of the market value, whichever amount is greater for each stock selling at $5.00 and above.

The requirements sound worse than they really are. For example, for 100 shares of XYZ selling at $3.00 per share, the requirement is:

$2.50 per share
$2.50 × 100 shares = $250

or

100% of the market value
$3.00 × 100 shares = $300

whichever is greater. $300 is more than $250, so $300 is the requirement.
Another example: for 100 XYZ at 10 ($1,000), the requirement is:

$5.00 per share
$5.00 × 100 shares = $500

or

30% of the market value
30% × $1000 = $300

whichever is greater. Therefore, $500 is the requirement.

The break point actually comes at 16.75, since 30 percent of 16.75 = $5.02, which is greater than $5.00 a share. Therefore, anytime you see a security selling above 16.75, the minimum maintenance requirement is a straight 30 percent of the market value. However, if the price is below 16.75, the special requirements for lower-priced stocks come into effect.

SAMPLE TRANSACTIONS

A customer's account contains the following long and short positions, and we want to determine the condition of the account with respect to the NYSE minimum maintenance requirements.

Margin Account				Short Account			
100	A	at 35	$3,500	100	X	at 20	$2,000
100	B	at 16	1,600	200	Y	at 10	2,000
200	C	at 22	4,400	100	Z	at 2	200
100	D	at 8	800				
Market value			$10,300	Short market value			$4,200
Debit balance			6,500	Credit balance			4,200
Equity			3,800				

	Req.	Eq.
	$2,575	$3,800
	600	0
	1,000	3,800
	250	
Total requirement	4,425	
Less total equity	−3,800	
	625	

This account is on NYSE minimum maintenance call for $625. We arrived at this figure through the following steps:

Step 1. The long market value is $10,300. The minimum maintenance requirement on the long side is 25 percent of the current market value, which is the first figure under the Req. column in the example ($2,575).

Step 2. When figuring the requirements on the short side, each security must be looked at separately if any is selling at less than 16.75. In the event all the securities were selling at 16.75 or above, just take 30 percent of the total short market value.

Step 3. However, neither is the case in our example. The first security short is 100 X at 20. The requirement is 30 percent of the market value ($600) or $5.00 per share ($500), whichever is greater. The greater of the two ($600) is the requirement (shown as the second figure under the Req. column in our example). The next security short is 200 Y at 10 per share. This requirement is again $5.00 per share ($1,000) or 30 percent of the market value ($600), whichever is greater. So $1,000 is the requirement (shown as the third figure under the Req. column). The last security short is 100 Z at 2. The requirement for this security is $2.50 per share ($250) or 100 percent of the market value ($200), again, whichever is greater. The minimum maintenance requirement for this security is $250 (fourth figure under the Req. column).

Step 4. Total requirement is the sum of all the requirements, both long and short. In the event the equity exceeded the requirement, there would have been excess over NYSE minimum maintenance requirements. However, this was not the case. The requirements exceeded the equity and the difference, $625, is the minimum NYSE maintenance call.

Notice the requirement on the 100 Z sold short at 2 exceeds the cost of covering the security. Recall that on the long side, a broker would never ask a customer for more than the full cost of the security. But a short position always has a higher degree of exposure. Consequently, requirements for short sales often exceed the market value of the security sold short.

Remember from Chapter 3 that there are four ways to meet a margin call:

1. Deposit the required funds.
2. Liquidate shares.
3. Deposit additional collateral.
4. Benefit from market appreciation.

The same four ways apply to the short side. However, meeting a margin call by liquidation on the short side is accomplished by purchasing the same security (buying in). There is one other difference. On the long side, meeting a margin call by liquidation requires selling securities with a value of four times the amount of the maintenance call. However, in this example covering or buying in 200 shares of Y at 10 would eliminate a dollar requirement of $1,000, bringing the account back into compliance with the NYSE maintenance requirement and, in fact, giving the account some excess over the minimum requirement.

Margin Account				**Short Account**			
100	A	at 35	$3,500	100	X	at 20	$2,000
100	B	at 16	1,600	100	Z	at 2	200
200	C	at 22	4,400				
100	D	at 8	800				

Market value	$10,300	Short market value	$2,200
Credit balance	6,500	Credit balance	2,200
Equity	3,800		

Req.	**Eq.**	
$2,575	$3,800	
600	0	
250	3,800	Total equity
	−3,425	
3,425	375	Excess over NYSE maint. requirement

The SMA now looks like this:

Date	**Debit**	**Credit**	**Balance**	**Explanation**
1/7/08		$1,000	$1,000	Cover 200 Y at 20

The proper entry to the SMA is to credit 50 percent of the cover price $1,000 and again, here is an example of an inflated SMA. Since the excess over the NYSE at this time is only $375, that would be the maximum amount that could be withdrawn.

SHORT SALE VERSUS THE BOX OR SHORT AGAINST THE BOX

Let us go back to the original definition of a short sale, found in the Securities Exchange Act of 1934: ". . . the sale of a security that you do not own or if you own it you do not intend to deliver it." Thus far, we have discussed only short sales where the customer does not own the security and is required to borrow it to complete the sale.

The term *short against the box* is a short sale where the customer owns the security and wishes to sell the same security short. First of all, why would someone wish to sell a security short when he or she owns it? Why not just sell it long? The primary reason is for tax purposes. A customer may have purchased a security that has since appreciated substantially. However, if the customer sells the security now, income tax must be paid on the profit in the current tax year, a year in which he has a substantial income. The customer anticipates that income will be lower next year, since he is planning to retire. If the sale could be made next year, this would result in a lower tax being paid on the profit. However, if he waits, he runs the risk that the market price of the security will decline, wiping out any profits. It would be in a case such as this that a customer would execute a short sale against the box.

A short sale against the box is handled exactly as a straight short sale as far as execution and operation. That is, the customer must be in position to borrow the security being sold. (The IRS has ruled that if a customer uses the long position to deliver versus the short, the position is considered closed out.) Further, the order must be marked as a short sale.

There was a major change in the tax law in 1997 concerning these types of transactions. The first change was that you could only carry over a gain or a loss to one year. Further, the short position must be closed out or covered by purchasing the short securities in the open market. You are no longer allowed to deliver your long position to the lender. In other words, you cannot close out your short with a journal entry. In addition, the position must be closed out prior to January 30 of the following year. After the cover, the open long position must remain in the account a minimum of 60 days in order to move the gain or loss to the following year.

Back to our customer who wants to sell short versus *the box* (the term means the long security owned by the customer is in the possession of the broker). Since marginal securities are financed, a portion of the customer's securities will be kept in the *active box*, as opposed to segregation (for fully paid for securities) where the securities are locked up for safekeeping. (A more detailed explanation of segregation will follow later on.)

When the short sale takes place, the customer will be both long 100 shares of A stock and short 100 shares of A stock, as a result of using borrowed shares for the delivery.

The customer's margin account prior to the short sale is as follows:

Margin Account—Long

100	A	40	$4,000
100	B	25	2,500
200	C	30	6,000
100	D	15	1,500

Market value	$14,000
Debit balance	8,000
Equity	6,000

There is no SMA balance.

Notice that this account is restricted, since the equity ($6,000) is below the current margin requirement ($7,000). After the short sale against the box, the account now appears as follows:

Margin Account				**Short Account**			
100	A	at 40	$4,000	100	A	at 40	$4,000
100	B	at 25	2,500				
200	C	at 30	6,000				
100	D	at 15	1,500				
Market value			$14,000	Short market value			$4,000
Debit balance			8,000	Credit balance			4,000
Equity			6,000				

The SMA now looks like this:

Date	**Debit**	**Credit**	**Balance**	**Explanation**
12/3/07		$2,000	$2,000	Short versus box 100 A

Notice that the long market value, debit balance, and equity remain unchanged. This is because the customer is still long 100 A at 40. Money did not come into or go out of the account.

In the short account is the new position short 100 A at 40. The proceeds of the short sale, which is being held as collateral by the lender of the securities, becomes the credit balance. The customer's SMA started off with zero and now has a credit balance of $2,000, or buying power of $4,000. Under Regulation T, if a customer is both long and short in the same security, the account is flat—that is, the net position is zero. Regulation T requires no margin and allows for the release of 50 percent of the sale proceeds ($2,000) to the SMA. However, there is an NYSE minimum maintenance requirement of 5 percent of the long side, and an obligation to mark the short side to the market.

Watch what happens if the market value of the securities in the account increases as follows:

Margin Account				**Short Account**			
100	A	at 50	$5,000	100	A	at 50	$5,000
100	B	at 30	3,000				
200	C	at 40	8,000				
100	D	at 20	2,000				
Market value			$18,000	Short market value			$5,000
Debit balance			8,000	Credit balance			4,000
Equity			10,000				

Remember, the customer is actually short and there is a lender of securities that is holding only $4,000 as collateral when the securities are actually worth $5,000. Therefore, there must be a mark to the market of $1,000 and an increase in the customer's credit balance of $1,000 to reflect how much the lender is actually holding. After the mark to the market, the account appears as follows:

Market value	$18,000	Short market value	$5,000
Debit balance	9,000	Credit balance	5,000
Equity	9,000		

Req.	Eq.
$6,500	$9,000
	−6,500
	$2,500

Here is the SMA:

Date	Debit	Credit	Balance	Explanation
12/3/07		$2,000	$2,000	Short versus box 100 A
12/10/07		500	2,500	Excess over Reg. T

The excess is $2,500; however, the SMA can only be credited an additional $500, bringing the balance up $2,500. Also note that the requirement is only $6,500, which represents 50 percent of the market value of 100 B, 200 C, and 100 D ($13,000). There is no Regulation T requirement on the 100 A at 50. There is an NYSE minimum maintenance requirement of 5 percent of the market value of A, and the short side must be kept marked to the market. This is why we increased the customer's debit balance and credit balance each by $1,000.

Refiguring this account for NYSE purposes, the following takes place:

Req.	Eq.	
$ 250	$9,000	
3,250	−3,500	
3,500	5,500	excess over NYSE minimum maintenance requirement

The $250 requirement represents the 5 percent maintenance on the long side of the short against the box position in A, and the $3,250 is the normal 25 percent of the market value of the remaining long securities ($13,000).

Prior to 1997, short versus the box positions were fairly common. Although they still exist, the number has diminished substantially.

PRIME BROKER

Thus far, we have discussed the mechanics of the short sale, initial and maintenance requirements, and closing out positions. However, a few more comments on short selling are timely at this point.

As you know, volumes on the various exchanges and the NASDAQ have increased tremendously in the past 20 years, and this is true for short selling as well. As of this writing, the *short interest* on the NYSE and AMEX was 9,653,015,623; on the NASDAQ 6,924,409,737.

The short interest is published monthly by *The Wall Street Journal* as of the fifteenth of each month. In addition to listing all of the shorts, it compares the current month with the previous month and indicates the change in volume plus or minus. Other highlighted areas are largest short positions, largest changes, largest percent increases, largest percent decreases, and largest short interest ratios, giving the average daily volume along with the number of days to cover based on that volume.

Studying the short interest is considered a valuable tool to the investor. Many investors feel that a large short position in a particular stock or group of securities is considered bearish and indicative of a downward movement in the price of the security or securities. However, for every single short position, there is one thing for certain. There has to be an eventual purchase of that security to close out that position. Purchases create demand, causing upward movement. When short sellers see upward movement, they tend to close out their positions causing more demand.

As a matter of information, short sellers do not hold their positions for any length of time. They take their profit and/or loss and close out the position and move on to another position. Perhaps this is why there is no such thing as a long-term capital gain on short sales. All profits are treated as income for tax purposes.

Another factor contributing to the increase in short selling has been the significant growth in recent years of hedge funds. Hedge funds are loosely regulated private partnerships that pool their investments. Often times, they are registered in low-tax offshore countries so that they can use derivatives and sell short. On-shore investment funds (mutual funds) are not permitted to use derivatives or sell short.

At best estimates, there are 8,000 hedge funds with assets under management of $1.5 trillion. At one time these funds were for very wealthy individuals. However, that has changed dramatically in recent years. Pension plans and other institutional investors, such as endowments and charitable organizations, have not only joined hedge funds, but also often substantially increased their investment allocations to these funds. In addition, some hedge fund managers are looking to Asia and its various emerging markets for additional growth.

As a result of the growing institutional trading and hedge funds, strategies such as short selling and use of options, discussed in Chapter 8, have increased substantially.

In the past few years, many hedge funds have gone out of business, causing huge losses to their investors. There was even a proposal by the Securities and Exchange Commission that hedge funds would have to be registered with the SEC. However, the proposal was defeated in the courts. Consequently, hedge funds remain, for the most part, unregulated.

Hedge funds offset the original purchase and reduce losses. The question arises, then, how can a hedge fund lose money? The reason is that many of these organizations engage in strategies so diverse and so multiple that many times they are not in a hedge position. Perhaps the purest definition of a hedge fund is combining leveraged use of borrowed funds to both go long securities and sell short. The result is that the hedge fund owns securities that it will profit from in a bullish market, and also has short positions to hedge against a bearish market.

Mutual funds are required by law to state in their prospectus their investment objectives and are bound by this statement. An investment objective can only be changed by a majority vote of the shareholders. Hedge funds, by contrast, do not have the same restrictions. In an adverse market, hedge funds can borrow to put up additional margin to wait out the adversity.

Mutual funds under the Investment Company Act of 1940 are required to make payment for any shares redeemed in 7 days. Hedge fund investors are usually prohibited from withdrawing for substantial periods of time—usually 6 months to one year.

This brief synopsis of hedge funds serves to provide you with the information that these organizations have greatly changed the use of margin trading and short selling. Individual investors and institutional investors have been using the same strategies. It's just that hedge funds' volume as to size of transactions and number of transactions has increased substantially over the past few years.

Competition among hedge funds is very keen. Fees as high as 1 to 3 percent of the value of the portfolio and sharing in 20 percent of the profits are common features.

Hedge fund investment strategies and techniques vary greatly, and these strategies are jealously guarded. In this regard, hedge funds use numerous brokers to take advantage of the expertise of the various brokers. This gave rise to the term *prime broker.*

Prime brokerage is a system developed by full-service firms to facilitate the clearance and settlement of security trades for substantial retail and institutional customers who are active market participants. Prime brokerage involves three distinct parties:

1. The prime broker
2. The executing broker
3. The customer

A little further background information might be helpful at this point. Regulation T currently requires an executing broker to treat its customers as its own explained below subject to all of the rules within Regulation T. The prime brokerage transactions are settled through the normal procedures in the prime broker's account at the executing broker (a broker/dealer account). However, this did not eliminate the executing broker's responsibilities under Regulation T. Under the current terms of Regulation T, the account at the executing broker is not a broker/dealer account, since the client is an agent of the prime broker.

Effective July 25, 1994, the Federal Reserve Board stated that it would not recommend that the Securities Exchange Commission take enforcement action if the executing broker and the prime broker treats the client's account as the executing broker as if it were a broker/dealer account if certain conditions exist. Listed are the margin/credit regulations that must be met:

- A broker/dealer acting as a prime broker must have a net capital of at least $1,500,000.
- Broker/dealers acting as executing brokers who clear prime broker transactions or broker/dealers clearing prime broker transactions on behalf of executing brokers must have capital of at lest $1,000,000.
- A prime broker may not settle prime broker trades on behalf of a customer, unless the customer keeps a minimum net equity with the prime broker of at least $500,000.
- Separate records must be kept by the prime broker identifying all customers using the prime broker arrangement.
- Trade information must be supplied to the prime broker by trade date + 1.
- The prime broker must be responsible to settle a particular transaction for the client with the executing broker unless it is disaffirmed by trade

date + 1. The executing broker must perform its own credit review to ensure that it knows the customer.

- The prime broker must keep records of all disaffirmed trades for three years.
- The executing broker must adhere to all of the applicable short sale provisions including determining that securities can be borrowed to deliver against the short sale.
- An executing broker must send directly to the customer a confirmation of each trade pursuant to Rule 10B-10. The executing broker may send the confirm to the customer in care of the prime broker if the customer so wishes. The prime broker must inform the customer in writing that the confirmation sent by the executing broker is available to the customer.
- The executing broker must keep and preserve records relating to the trades placed with the executing broker.
- When a prime broker disaffirms, a cancellation notice must be sent to the customer to offset the notification sent on trade date + 1. The executing broker must send a new confirmation to the customer.
- Rule 11(d)(1) prohibits an executing broker from extending or arranging for a prime broker to extend credit on a security sold by the executing broker to the customer if the executing broker was a member of a selling syndicate within the prior thirty (30) days; however, the prime broker may extend credit on such a security in a margin account previously established independently by the customer if this credit was not otherwise arranged by the executing broker.
- The prime broker must treat the customer for all purposes including Regulation T, SEC Rules 15c3–1, 15c3–3, 17A-3 and 17A-4.

CHAPTER FIVE QUESTIONS

1. Before securities can be sold short, which of the following are required?
   a. The broker must be in a position to borrow the securities.
   b. The order must be marked short.
   c. If listed, you are not subject to the up-tick requirement.
   d. All of the above.

2. What is the NYSE minimum maintenance requirement on a short position 1,000 shares of ABC at $1.00?
   a. $500

    b. $2,500

    c. $250

    d. $1,000

3. A short sale against the box of $10,000 requires how much for Regulation T?

    a. $5,000

    b. $2,500

    c. $1,000

    d. 0

4. The covering of a short sale for $7,500 will release how much to the customer's SMA?

    a. $3,750

    b. no release on the covering of a short

    c. $2,250

    d. $7,500

5. What is the NYSE minimum maintenance requirement on a short position of 100 ABC at 50?

    a. $2,500

    b. $1,500

    c. $1,250

    d. $5,000

6. The customer has a short market value of $35,000 and a total credit balance of $50,000. What is the equity in this account?

    a. $15,000

    b. $85,000

    c. $30,000

    d. $60,000

7. (Same account as in Question 6.) This account would be classified as a:

    a. short account.

    b. cash account.

    c. margin account.

    d. restricted margin account.

8. The maximum loss on any short position is?

    a. the current short market value.

    b. 50 percent of the short market value.

    c. unlimited.

    d. 140 percent of current short market value.

9. An initial transaction in a customer's margin account is a short sale of 100 XYZ at 5. What is the required deposit?
   a. $250
   b. $2,000
   c. $500
   d. $1,000

10. A customer is short 100 ABC and a 3-for-2 stock split is declared by ABC company. The customer is now short how many shares?
    a. 200 shares
    b. 100 shares
    c. 150 shares
    d. 50 shares

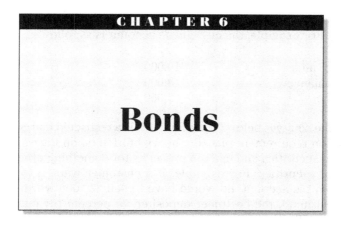

CHAPTER 6

Bonds

Bonds are a vital part of the securities industry and, in total, constitute a far larger market than stocks, which gets all the attention. The news media always refer to the Dow Jones averages and trading volume on the New York Stock Exchange, but the dollar volume of bond trading dwarfs the value of stock trading. We will discuss only a few of the many types of bonds issued today, since our focus is on bonds in the margin account. Here are the categories, as far as margin trading is concerned:

- Convertibles into a margin security
- Nonequity securities, which Reg. T calls debt securities
- Over-the-counter (OTC) margin debt securities (marginable securities).
- Exempted securities, which include U.S. government obligations and political subdivisions of the United States (states, counties, cities, etc.), more commonly referred to as municipals or *munis*
- Certain foreign sovereign debt securities

Prior to getting into the nuts and bolts of trading bonds in the margin account, let's look at some background information. In Chapter 3, we explained that when the equity in a margin account falls below the existing margin requirement, the account becomes restricted. Years ago, it was subject to the 50 percent retention requirement. The effect of this retention requirement was to limit the amount of money that could be withdrawn on sales of securities in a restricted margin account. When the retention requirement went into effect, the initial margin requirement was 90 percent. For example, the customer's account is as follows:

Market value	$10,000
Debit balance	3,000
Equity	7,000

Since the equity is below 90 percent, this is a restricted margin account. The retention requirement placed a heavy burden on an investor who desired to sell securities and use the proceeds for something other than the purchase of securities. For example, if a customer wanted to withdraw $10,000 from his account, he would have to sell $20,000 worth of securities. Keep in mind, the customer deposited 90 percent for purchase and received only 50 percent on the sale. It wasn't long before a loophole was discovered. The customer would sell $10,000 worth of securities and purchase $10,000 worth of U.S. government securities (also called *exempt securities* because they are exempt from the various rules and regulations, including this 50 percent retention requirement). Consequently, the subsequent sale of the Treasury securities would release the entire $10,000, and the cost to the customer would be just the additional commission on the purchase and sale of the Treasury securities—and commissions on Treasury securities are very small.

Needless to say, when the Federal Reserve discovered this practice, it took steps to close this loophole. It established two new accounts: the special convertible debt securities account and the special bond account. By establishing a separate bond account for Treasury and municipals as well as listed corporate debt securities, the loophole would be closed. The reason for establishing an entirely separate account for the listed convertible bond was that this security is a hybrid—part bond, part equity—because of its ability to change from a debt instrument into an equity instrument.

The special convertible debt security account and the special bond account were eliminated on November 23, 1983, and these securities once again became eligible for trading in the customer's margin account. Having these extra accounts was cumbersome and confusing. In addition, these accounts were not permitted to have SMAs attached to them, again requiring journal entries to preserve buying power.

Debt securities which are convertible into margin securities now have the same margin requirements as listed equity securities—50 percent on initial purchases, 50 percent release on sales, and the same entries to the customer's SMA. In fact, the New York Stock Exchange has the same minimum maintenance requirement for both: 25 percent of the current market value.

TABLE 6.1	NYSE Initial and Maintenance Requirements on U.S. Government obligations

Years to Maturity	NYSE Requirement (% of Market Value)
Less than 1 year	1%
1 year but less than 3 years	2%
3 years but less than 5 years	3%
5 years but less than 10 years	4%
10 years but less than 20 years	5%
20 years or more	6%

The remaining debt instruments we will discuss are nonconvertible corporate bonds and exempt securities. Exempt securities include direct obligations of the U.S. government such as Treasury bills, Treasury notes, and Treasury bonds, or any agency guaranteed as to interest or principal by the U.S. government. In addition, exempt securities include municipal bonds (munis) issued by political subdivisions of the United States, such as New York State, New Jersey, California, or any other city or state obligation are exempt securities.

U.S. GOVERNMENT SECURITIES

As stated earlier, direct obligations of the U.S. government are exempt and are not subject to Regulation T. However, the NYSE has initial and minimum maintenance requirements that went into effect on September 1, 1987. These requirements are a sliding scale, requiring less as the instrument approaches maturity. Table 6.1 gives the requirement for Treasury bills and interest-bearing notes and bonds.

ZERO-COUPON GOVERNMENT OBLIGATIONS

Bonds usually have a face amount or principal of $1,000 at maturity, as well as a fixed amount of interest usually payable semiannually. This interest is either paid directly by the issuer to the owner of the bond, if it is a registered bond, or the owner clips interest coupons attached to the bonds and presents them to a paying agent to collect the interest.

TABLE 6.2	Initial and Maintenance Requirements on Zero-Coupon Government Obligations

Years to Maturity	NYSE Requirement (% of Market Value)
5 or more	3% of principal
More than 5 but less than 10	3% of principal or 4% of market (whichever is greater)
More than 10 but less than 20	3% of principal or 5% of market (whichever is greater)
More than 20	3% of principal or 6% of market (whichever is greater)

The latter may be a registered bond (in the name of the owner) but is usually a bearer bond. (The holder of the bond is the owner.)[1]

A zero-coupon government obligation is a government note or bond where all the coupons have been removed. Therefore, no interest will be paid during the life of the security. At maturity, it will be redeemed at the face value. Since no interest will be paid, this instrument trades at a deep discount from its face value, depending on the number of years to maturity. In many respects it is like a savings bond; you pay $25 for it but get back $50 at maturity. See Table 6.2.

All bonds, whether corporate, government, or municipal, trade at a percentage of par that is $1,000. A price of 100 means 100 percent of par value, or $1,000. A quote on a Treasury note may be "bid, 98.4, ask 98.8." That is a percentage of $1,000 on the bid—in this case, 98.4/32 percent of $1,000, or $981.25. Government notes and bonds trade in 32nds; corporate bonds trade in decimals.

Example: A customer purchases $10,000 of zero-coupon U.S. Treasury bonds maturing 2/15/25, selling at 32 (total cost: $3,200) in a margin account with existing positions as indicated in the following chart. The requirement would be 3 percent of principal ($300) or 5 percent of the market value ($160), whichever is greater (in this case, $300). After the purchase, the account would appear as follows:

100	B	35	$3,500
200	C	40	$8,000
100	D	50	$5,000
100	E	35	$3,500

---

[1]Bearer bonds over the years have diminished substantially; however, there are still a few remaining.

10,000 U.S. Treasury bonds 2/15/25 at 32 3,200:

Market value	$23,200
Debit balance	15,200
Equity	8,000

The SMA looks like this:

Date	Debit	Credit	Balance	Explanation
1/15/08		$2,000		Sale 100 A at 40

Notice that there is no entry (debit) to the customer's SMA, and no Regulation T call was issued, because there is no Federal Reserve requirement. The $300 requirement is an NYSE initial and maintenance requirement and is already in the account.

Req.	Eq.	
$5,000	$8,000	
300	−5,300	
$5,300	$2,700	excess over NYSE req.

The $5,000 requirement is 25 percent of the current market value of the equity securities that were already in the margin account. The $300 requirement is 3 percent of the principal amount on the newly purchased zero-coupon government obligation. Although no deposit was required on the purchase of the zero-coupon government obligation, nothing will be released to the SMA when it is sold, either. However, you may always recompute the account and give the customer any excess over Reg. T.

The same principle applies when purchasing other direct government obligations: There are no Federal Reserve requirements and the NYSE requirements are the same as those stated earlier.

Most investors would not purchase a large amount of government securities using the minimum requirements, because the interest charged on the debit balance would exceed the yield on the security. However, a customer might have $100,000 fully paid for 9–1/4 percent Treasury notes due May 2010 trading at par and might need to borrow $95,000 for a business venture for six months. The customer may very well use these securities as collateral.

MUNICIPALS

Generally, municipal securities fall into one of two categories. The first, *general obligations*, are backed by the full faith and credit of the issuer.

The second, *revenue bonds,* are not backed by the municipalities, but by the revenue generated by a particular facility, such as the Triborough Bridge and Tunnel Authority bonds, or the Meadowlands Sports Complex. Neither of these bonds is guaranteed by their respective states of New York and New Jersey. The money needed to meet the interest and principal payments to the bondholders must come from the revenue generated by operating each facility. Should the revenue not be sufficient to pay the interest and principal, the bonds would go into default.

Remember, municipal securities are also classified as exempt, and no requirement is imposed by the Federal Reserve or Regulation T. However, the NYSE has initial and maintenance requirements, which are 15 percent of the market value or 7 percent of the principal (whichever amount is greater). When do these initial requirements take effect? If a customer purchased 10 M ($10,000) NYC 8–1/2 of 2/15/10 at 87, a requirement is established for 15 percent of the market value ($1,305) or 7 percent of the principal ($700), whichever is greater (in this case, $1,305).

The requirement for municipals will usually be 15 percent of the market value. This is because in order for the 7 percent requirement to be the larger of the two, the market value of the bond would have to be 46.62 or lower, which would mean the interest rate would be around 2 percent, and the bond would have had to be issued a long time ago. Very few such bonds are around. However, should interest rates rise sharply, bond prices will fall, and the 7 percent of principal could become a factor.

Let's look at our margin account and see what happens with a purchase of 10 NYC 8–1/2 of 2/15/10 at 87.

100	B	35	$3,500
200	C	40	$8,000
100	D	50	$5,000
100	E	35	$3,500
10M	U.S. Treasury Bonds 2/15/25 at 32		$3,200
10M	NYC 8–1/2 2/15/10 at 87		$8,700

Market value	$31,900
Debit balance	23,900
Equity	8,000

Now the SMA is as follows:

Date	Debit	Credit	Balance	Explanation
1/15/08		$2,000		Sale 100 A at 40

Again, no change occurs in the SMA because there is no Regulation T requirement. However, looking at the size of the customer's debit balance, is it possible that the account may require funds for the New York Stock Exchange?

Req.	Eq.	
$5,000	$8,000	
300	−6,605	
$1,305	$1,395	excess over NYSE req.
$6,605		

This account is fine, since there is an excess of $1,395. The requirements were arrived at by taking 25 percent of the market value of the four stocks (25% × $20,000 = $5,000), plus 3 percent of the zero-coupon government obligation (3% × $10,000 = $300), plus 15 percent of the market value of the municipal security, (15% × $8,700 = $1,305).

Carrying this a step further, let's assume the market value of the securities increases as follows:

100	B		55	$5,500
200	C		43	$8,600
100	D		60	$6,000
100	E		41	$4,100
10M	U.S. Treasury bonds 2/15/25 at 42			$4,200
10M	NYC 8–1/2 2/15/10 at 92			$9,200

Market value	$37,600
Debit balance	23,900
Equity	13,700

Now the SMA is as follows:

Date	Debit	Credit	Balance	Explanation
1/15/08		$2,000	$2,000	Sale 100 A at 40

And recomputing for Regulation T:

Req.	Eq.	
$12,100	$13,700	
	−12,100	
	$1,600	excess over Reg. T

Notice that under Req. column we are only using a figure of $12,100. This represents 50 percent of the market value of the stock in the account. The $10,000 of U.S. Treasury bonds and the $10,000 of NYC bonds are exempt securities having no Regulation T requirement. In addition, since the current balance in the SMA is $2,000, there would not be any additional entry to the SMA.

NONCONVERTIBLE CORPORATE BONDS

Nonconvertible bonds sometimes are referred to as *straight corporate debt securities.* Nonconvertible bonds are eligible for purchase in the margin account. Margin requirements for these securities are a bit odd. Regulation T allows brokers (creditors) to establish their own margin requirements for straight corporate bonds and accepts whatever that requirement is as the Fed's. Therefore, one broker may charge 40 percent of the market value and another broker 25 percent of the market value. However, the NYSE also has initial and maintenance requirements for nonconvertible bonds: 20 percent of the market value or 7 percent of the principal, whichever amount is greater. These, then, become the minimum requirements. Effectively, a broker could require more than the NYSE minimum, but no less.

For any listed bond selling above 35, the requirement will be 20 percent of the market value. The requirement for any bond selling below 35 will be 7 percent of the principal or face amount. At 35, the requirements are the same—$70, based on a $1,000 bond.

Back to our customer, currently as follows:

100	B	55	$5,500
200	C	43	$8,600
100	D	60	$6,000
100	E	41	$4,100
10M	U.S. Treasury bonds 2/15/25 at 42		$4,200
10M	NYC 8–1/2 2/15/10 at 92		$9,200

Market value	$37,600
Debit balance	23,900
Equity	13,700

The SMA looks like this:

Date	Debit	Credit	Balance	Explanation
1/15/08		$2,000	$2,000	Sale 100 A at 40

If this customer now purchases 10 Ford Motor credit bonds 8–1/2 due 2010 at 87.50, the account will look like this:

100	B		55	$5,500
200	C		43	$8,600
100	D		60	$6,000
100	E		41	$4,100
10M	U.S. Treasury bonds 2/15/25 at 42			$4,200
10M	NYC 8–1/2 2/15/10 at 92			$9,200
10M	Ford Motor Credit 8–1/2 2010 at 87.50			$8,750

Market value	$46,350
Debit balance	32,650
Equity	13,700

Now this purchase has a Regulation T requirement of the greater of 20 percent of the market value: $1,750; or 7 percent of the principal ($700). $1,750 is the NYSE requirement, but because of the language in Regulation T, it becomes a Federal call. Since funds are available in the SMA, the entry is as follows:

The SMA looks like this:

Date	Debit	Credit	Balance	Explanation
1/15/08		$2,000	$2,000	Sale 100 A at 40
1/28/08	$1,750		$250	Pur. 10M Ford

Look at our account. Again, that debit looks large, and the account should be refigured for NYSE.

Req.	Eq.	
$6,050	$13,700	
300	−9,480	
$1,380	$4,220	excess over NYSE min.
1,750		maintenance requirement
$9,480		

All we are doing is taking each item separately. The $6,050 represents 25 percent of the current market value of the equity securities (the stocks) in the margin account; $300 is the requirement of 3 percent of the principal amount of the zero-coupon government obligation; $1,380 is the requirement of 15 percent of the market value of the municipal bond; and $1,750 is the requirement of 20 percent of the market value of the listed corporate debt security. Remember that 20 percent of the market value of the corporate bond is both a Fed initial requirement and an NYSE minimum maintenance requirement.

Effective September 15, 1988, the Federal Reserve Board announced that Regulation T had been amended to allow U.S. brokers to extend credit on certain foreign sovereign debt securities. The effect of this amendment is to allow loan value on long-term debt securities issued or guaranteed as a general obligation by a foreign sovereign government. In order for these securities to be eligible, the foreign sovereign debt instruments must be rated by Standard & Poor's or Moody's and given one of the two highest ratings, AA or AAA. The securities in question may be treated the same as OTC margin bonds.

According to Regulation T, good-faith loan value is sufficient. However, members of the NYSE or NASD would be subject to the greater of 20 percent of the current market value or 7 percent of the principal of the bond in question.

The following is from Section 220.0 (Definitions) of the amendment.

> *(4) A debt security issued or guaranteed as a general obligation by the government of a foreign country, its provinces, states, or cities, or a super-national entity, if at the time of the extension of credit one of the following is rated in one of the two highest rating categories by a nationally recognized statistical rating organization:*
>
> > *(i) the issue,*
> > *(ii) the issuer or guarantor (implicitly), or*
> > *(iii) other outstanding unsecured long-term debt securities issued or guaranteed by the government or entity.*

CHAPTER SIX QUESTIONS

1. The NYSE minimum requirements for the long position in listed convertible bonds is:

   a. $2,000.
   b. 50 percent of the market value.
   c. no NYSE requirements.
   d. 25 percent or the market value.

2. A purchase of a Treasury bill has a Regulation T requirement of:

   a. 5 percent of the principal amount.
   b. 1 percent of the market value.

   c. 15 percent of the market value.

   d. no Regulation T requirement.

3. The purchase of a NYC general obligation bond has a NYSE requirement of:

   a. 15 percent of the market value or 7 percent of the principal whichever is greater.

   b. 25 percent of the market value.

   c. 5 percent of the principal amount.

   d. no requirement; it is classified as an exempt security.

4. If a customer deposits a fully paid-for Treasury note maturing in two years the broker may lend the customer:

   a. 50 percent of the market value.

   b. 98 percent of the market value.

   c. 3 percent of the market value.

   d. 25 percent of the market value.

5. Exempt securities are:

   a. direct obligations of the United States.

   b. municipal bonds.

   c. an agency guaranteed as to principal or interest by the United States.

   d. all of the above.

6. A purchase of a municipal revenue bond requires a deposit of:

   a. 100 percent of the market value.

   b. 15 percent of the market value or 7 percent of the principal, whichever amount is greater.

   c. 50 percent of the market value.

   d. 25 percent of the market value.

7. The settlement date on purchases of U.S. government obligations is:

   a. five business days.

   b. seven business days.

   c. the next business day.

   d. two business days after the trade date, known as a skip settlement.

8. A purchase of a zero-coupon government bond maturing in 22 years requires a NYSE maintenance requirement of:

   a. no requirement.

   b. 3 percent of the principal or 6 percent of the market value, whichever is greater.

   c. 3 percent of the principal.

   d. 50 percent of the market value.

9. A customer purchases $100,000 of Canadian debt securities. The required Regulation T margin is:

   a. 20 percent of the market value or 7 percent of the principal amount, whichever is greater.
   b. full payment is required.
   c. 50 percent—same as listed securities.
   d. no margin, treat the same as U.S. government obligations

10. Foreign sovereign debt must be rated by a recognized investment service in which rating:

   a. AA or A
   b. the top four rating, making them bank quality.
   c. AA or AAA.
   d. A or above.

CHAPTER 7

Miscellaneous Categories

This chapter discusses areas that the margin department is responsible for, but are either dealt with infrequently or have been automated.

WHEN-ISSUED AND WHEN-DISTRIBUTED TRANSACTIONS

A *when-issued* transaction is a trade in a security that has not yet been issued and in reality is a *when-as-and-if-issued* transaction. There is no guarantee that a security trading on a when-issued basis will in fact be issued. A security will be traded on a when-issued basis in several situations. If a company announces plans to split the stock, the old security will trade at one price and the new security (if it were a two-for-one split) would trade at one-half the price of the old security. While the plan for the split has been announced, it still must be approved by the stockholders, the SEC, and so on. When one company announces plans to merge with another, the new security often starts trading on a when-issued basis. There have been times when the deal was all set to be completed and the U.S. Justice Department stepped in at the last moment and declared the merger in violation of antitrust laws. When this happens, the when-issued contract is canceled and the deal is canceled. Any profits that a customer may have are eliminated, as well as any losses. Once the deal has been approved by all parties, however, the securities start trading on a *regular-way* basis. When-issued securities are *unissued* and are referred to as such under Regulation T.

An interesting specific example of when-issued trading was the break-up of the American Telephone and Telegraph Company. Under government orders to divest itself of local operating companies, AT&T spun off the following companies:

- NYNEX
- Pacific Telesis
- Southwestern Bell
- U.S. West
- Ameritech
- BellSouth
- Bell Atlantic

Because of the size of this company and the millions of shares involved, these seven new companies traded on a when-issued basis for a number of months, until the new securities became available.

In a customer's cash account, purchases of when-issued securities may be made, but full payment is not required until five (5) business days after the security is available for delivery (begin trading regular way). However, there are deposit requirements under NYSE Rule 431. The purchase of a when-issued contract in a customer's cash account requires a deposit of 25 percent or $2,000, whichever is greater. In the event full payment is less than $2,000, full payment must be received promptly (three business days). Consequently, a customer who purchases $10,000 of when-issued securities in a cash account would require no funds as far as Regulation T is concerned, but would be required to deposit $2,500 to satisfy the NYSE requirement. This is the same as the initial requirement of $2,000 and minimum maintenance requirement of 25 percent for a margin account. In fact, a customer may be able to purchase a when-issued security without depositing any additional funds. Suppose a customer had existing accounts as follows:

Customer's Accounts

Customer's Cash Account
Market value (long) Securities	$20,000

Customer's Margin Account
Market value	$10,000
Debit balance	5,000
Equity	5,000

If this customer purchased $10,000 of when-issued securities in a cash account, no deposit would be required since the required funds are already in the account.

	Req.	**Eq.**	
25% of M.V in cash acct.	$5,000	$20,000	equity in cash account
25% req. on when issued	2,500	+5,000	equity in margin account
25% req. on margin acct.	2,500	25,000	total equity
	$10,000	−10,000	total requirement
		$15,000	excess over NYSE req.

In our example, the customer has an excess of $15,000 over the NYSE requirement.

A word of caution: Although in the previous example the deposit of $2,500 would not have to be made, full cash payment is still required five business days after the security starts trading on a regular-way basis. In the event the customer sells the when-issued securities prior to depositing the full cash payment, the cash account becomes frozen for 90 calendar days.

Now let's assume that after our customer purchases a when-issued security for $10,000, the price increased to $11,000, and he/she wishes to sell it while it is still trading on a when-issued basis. To avoid the 90-day freeze, the customer must now deposit the entire $10,000, representing the full cash payment. After the sale, the only funds that could be returned to the customer would be the deposit of $10,000. The $1,000, representing the profit, would be retained until the third business day after the security started trading on a regular-way basis, which would be the settlement date for the when-issued contract.

The reason for the retention of the profit is the possibility of the contract being canceled. If it was canceled, the $1,000 profit would be eliminated. Keep in mind that when-issued contracts do not settle until they are actually issued. Suppose the price drops to $9,000, and the customer wishes to sell it while it is still trading on a when-issued basis. To avoid the 90-day freeze, the customer would have to deposit the full cost ($10,000). If the sale was made for $9,000, the release to the customer would be $9,000. The $1,000 loss would be held by the broker until the settlement date. In the event the when-issued security was canceled, the $1,000 would be returned to the customer and no loss would be sustained.

Purchases of when-issued securities in a customer's margin account are treated the same as any other issued, listed security. Section 220.4(b)(3) of Regulation T states: "The required margin on a net long or short commitment in an unissued security is the margin that would be required if the security were an issued margin security." Therefore, purchases in the customer's margin account require a deposit of 50 percent of the market value. This is the one instance that cash account requirements are lower than margin account requirements. The procedure of retaining any profits or losses until the security goes the regular way is exactly the same for margin accounts as for cash accounts.

Marks to the Market

When-issued securities are also subject to marks to the market. This is particularly true when the when-issued contract will be open for a long period of time. The break-up of American Telephone and Telegraph into new companies resulted in the new companies trading on a when-issued basis for nine months. A mark to the market occurs when the price changes. In our first example, the customer purchased $10,000 of a when-issued security, and the price increased to $11,000. The broker would charge or debit the selling broker $1,000 to protect the customer. In the event the selling broker went out of business, the buying broker would have sufficient funds to repurchase the security and make the customer whole. A mark to the market against us would occur if, after we purchased a when-issued contract, the market value declined.

When-Distributed Securities

When-distributed securities are far less common than when-issued securities. The only difference is that a when-distributed security is, in fact, an issued security, just not distributed as yet. This transaction occurs when a company that owns another company decides to distribute the securities to its shareholders. The physical requirement of printing certificates and breaking them down into the proper denominations takes time. Consequently, the security will trade on a when-distributed basis. They are treated the same as a when-issued security as far as purchases and sales in the customers' cash and margin accounts. Physical securities are still with us. However, the vast majority are being held at DTCC. Consequently, the distribution process is much faster and would not be the problem it was years ago.

SEGREGATION OF CUSTOMERS' SECURITIES

One of the most important rules, not only from the brokers' and regulatory agencies' standpoint, but also from the customers' standpoint, is the requirement that the broker segregate customers' securities.

As you may know, one of the services that a broker performs is keeping custody of customers' securities. The advantages of such a service are numerous. The securities are in a safe place; the securities are more likely to be delivered promptly when sales are made, dividends and other distributions are easier to distribute; and the customers' securities are insured by the federally chartered organization known as Securities Investors' Protection Corporation. Most brokers don't charge a custody fee for this service. However, the broker is in a good position. If the security is sold, it will probably be sold by the broker holding the security, thereby assuring the broker a commission on the sale. Although there are definite advantages to holding the customers' securities, brokers must comply with certain restrictions.

Fully paid-for customers' securities must be completely segregated. *Segregated* is the term used on Wall Street for safekeeping or locking up customers' securities. Therefore, if customer purchases securities in a cash account, when the securities are received and paid for, they must be identified as to whom they belong and then placed into segregation. Fully paid-for securities must be placed into segregation, even if they are to remain in *street name* (held in the broker's name as opposed to the actual individual's name). In this regard, each broker must maintain a *stock record*—a record that shows the position and location of all the securities that the broker is responsible for. This record is truly the heart and lungs of the brokerage operation.

REVIEW OF CUSTOMERS' ACCOUNTS

Brokerage firms are subject to examination by each of the following organizations:

New York Stock Exchange (if members)

National Association of Security Dealers

The Securities and Exchange Commission

In addition, they must submit to an audit once a year by an outside certified public accountant, and are responsible for internal audits.

Each examining staff will first check the brokerage firm's net capital and then its stock record to see if customers' fully paid-for securities are in fact segregated as required. Failure to comply with this requirement can lead to substantial fines and suspensions.

What about securities that are not fully paid for? A portion of the securities held in a margin account may be used to finance the debit as follows:

Customer's Margin Account

Market value	$35,000
Debit balance	15,000
Equity	20,000

In most instances, a broker carrying this account would finance the customer's debit balance by going to a bank and borrowing the $15,000. Brokers borrow from banks at what is known as the *broker's call rate*—a secured demand loan, hence the name. This loan is secured by pledging a portion of the customer's securities.

The actual segregation rule requires the broker to segregate anything in excess of 140 percent of the debit balance. In other words, the broker must segregate, or lock up, $14,000 of the customer's securities. The remaining $21,000 (140% × $15,000 = $21,000) may be placed as collateral with the bank. The reason for this rather odd percentage is that banks will lend from 70 percent to 75 percent of the value of the security, depending on its quality. Therefore, in our example, the brokerage firm's stock record would show $21,000 in bank loan and $14,000 in segregation. This rule is aimed at protecting the customer. Let's look at our account again:

Customer's Margin Account

Market value	$35,000
Debit balance	15,000
Equity	20,000

Location of customer's securities:

Bank Loan	Segregation or Vault
$21,000	$14,000

In the event that the brokerage house went bankrupt, the bank holding the securities securing the loan of $15,000 would liquidate the securities to obtain payment of their $15,000 loan. The remaining $6,000 would be turned over the liquidator. The remaining $14,000 of securities that were properly placed in segregation would give the customer a combined total of $20,000, which is exactly the customer's equity or ownership in the account.

In this regard, when a customer opens a margin account, he must sign a margin agreement, which describes in detail the various requirements and responsibilities. Upon reading the agreement, there is a provision for the rehypothecation of customer securities. *Rehypothecation* means to repledge.

In the previous example, the repledging of $21,000 of the customer's securities to the bank to secure the loan of $15,000 is also known as rehypothecation of the customer's securities.

Earlier we mentioned stock loans. Remember, when a broker lends securities for stock loans, the broker usually gets 100 percent of the market value as collateral. Using our example:

Customer's Margin Account

Market value	$35,000
Debit balance	15,000
Equity	20,000

If our broker lends the customer's securities for a stock loan and receives 100 percent of the market value, the stock record for the customer's securities would show the following:

Stock Loan	**Segregation or Vault**
$15,000	$20,000

Since the broker received $15,000 in cash to collateralize the loan of $15,000 of securities, our broker would now be required to segregate the remaining $20,000 of securities.

INTEREST CHARGES

As you can imagine, a margin account is a credit account where a customer pays for a portion of the securities and the broker, referred to as a *creditor* under Regulation T, finances the remainder. As we have stated, the current requirement under Regulation T is 50 percent. This means that a purchase of $10,000 of securities requires a deposit of $5,000. The broker is financing the remaining $5,000—a loan to the customer.

As a general rule, brokers must borrow the money from a bank to finance this purchase. As previously stated in this chapter, brokers borrow money from banks at the *broker's call rate* and then add a minimum of one half of 1 percent when charging a customer interest on the loan made to him. For debit balances under $50,000, generally the interest rate charged will be more.

The customer must be advised as to how much the charges will be when due and how they must be paid. This is usually done in the customer's margin account agreement. There are several rules, laws, and regulations that require this information to be disclosed: Securities and Exchange Commission Rule 10 (b), Regulation Z of the Federal Reserve System, and the Truth in Lending Law of 1968. These rules, regulations, and laws are lengthy, wordy, and complicated, but we will try to simplify them.

Interest rates are based on an annual rate, and interest due is calculated by using the following formula:

$$\text{Interest} = \text{Principal} \times \text{Rate} \times \text{Time}$$

The amount of interest charged is reflected in the customer's monthly statement. This statement reflects all the customer's transactions for the previous month, along with the current holdings—both long and short. In a statement for a margin account, there is a debit charge titled *interest* or *interest charges*, which will increase the debit balance by that amount. The date that interest is charged will vary from firm to firm. Usually the interest is charged on the fifteenth of the month and the statement cut-off date may be some time after that—for example, the twentieth of each month. Let's assume our customer's margin account has the following balances:

Market value	$100,000
Debit balance	60,000
Equity	40,000

First, note that in our example the account is restricted. The debit balance is in excess of $50,000; therefore, the broker is only charging the minimum interest of one half of 1 percent above the broker's call rate. If broker's call rate is currently 7 percent, when we add 0.5 percent, the actual charge to the customer will be 7.5 percent. Therefore, on the fifteenth of the month the broker would increase the customer's debit as follows:

$$\$375 \left(\$60,000 \times 7.5\% \times \frac{30}{360} \text{ days} \right)$$

The broker's actual cost of fund was

$$\$350 \left(\$60,000 \times 7\% \times \frac{30}{360} \text{ days} \right)$$

The broker's mark-up is minimal: $25 per month. However, where the broker can really make money is through the stock loan program. By using available securities in house and getting 100 percent of the market value in cash for a stock loan, the broker is now able to finance the customer's debit balance.

Instead of borrowing from the bank, the broker may use stock loans and get the money "free" and charge the margin customer the same 7.5 percent. Since the broker has no cost of funds, the $375 charged in this example is pure profit.

The customer's account after the charge will look like this:

Market value	$100,000
Debit balance	60,375
Equity	39,625

The charge of $375 would not create a Fed call requiring the customer to deposit additional funds, even though the increase in the debit further restricts the margin account.

MARGIN ON NEW ISSUES

The Securities and Exchange Commission has ruled that credit cannot be extended on new issues until 30 days after the syndicate was closed. This means that brokers are not allowed to finance or let their customers buy new issues on margin—for good reason. Underwriters are anxious to sell the securities they are distributing in order to close out the syndicate and get on to another deal. Should a particular underwriting be going poorly, an underwriter might be tempted to convince customers to take more securities than they should by placing them in the customers' margin accounts. The SEC's ruling prevents this occurrence.

This created a problem on certain investment company securities. Closed-end investment companies presented no problem if they were marginable securities and were over 30 days old after the syndicate was closed; they would be eligible for margin. However, open-end investment companies (mutual funds) presented a different problem. Purchases of these securities are direct from the fund itself. Consequently, the SEC ruled that these purchases are a continuing *new issue*. However, if a customer has held the securities for 30 days, they may be transferred from the customer's cash account (where they would have been required to be purchased) to the customer's margin account, where the broker may extend the 50 percent loan value on the securities.

However, there is one exception: If the customer purchased open-end investment shares (mutual funds) elsewhere (through another broker), the shares are immediately eligible for the margin account upon transfer to the other broker and may have credit extended on them.

DAY TRADES

A *day trade* is the purchase and sale of the same security on the same day. Under Regulation T, no deposit is required if there is no increase in the customer's debit balance at the end of the day. Assume the customer's account is as follows:

Market value	$30,000
Debit balance	17,000
Equity	13,000

If this customer purchased $10,000 of securities in this account and sold the same $10,000 of securities later in the day with neither a profit nor a loss, there would be no Regulation T requirement.

Account after the purchase of $10,000

Market value	$40,000
Debit balance	27,000
Equity	13,000

Account after the sale of $10,000

Market value	$30,000
Debit balance	17,000
Equity	13,000

As you can see, no change occurs in the customer's debit balance from the beginning of the day to the end. Consequently, there is no Regulation T requirement.

The chance that a customer would buy and sell a security on one day with no change in price is remote. However, if a loss of $1,000 or less were incurred, this would constitute a Regulation T call. But the amount may be waived at the broker's discretion. Profits may be placed in the customer's SMA.

The major regulatory agencies governing day trades are the NASD and the New York Stock Exchange, which have two different requirements, one for non-day traders (they are required to have a minimum equity in their respective margin accounts of at least $2,000). The other is for a *pattern day trader.*

Requirements for a Pattern Day Trader

The regulatory agencies consider a pattern day trader a customer who executes four or more day trades within five business days. However, if the number of day trades is 6 percent or less of the total trades for the five-business-day period, the customer will be classified as a nonpattern day trader.

The minimum equity requirement for a pattern day trader is $25,000. This amount must be maintained at all times.

Day trading buying power means the equity in a customer's account at the close of business of the previous day, less any maintenance margin requirement as preceded in NYSE Rule 431 and NASD Rule 2520, multiplied by 4 for equity securities.

Market value	$100,000
Debit balance	55,000
Equity	45,000

Recompute the account for day trading buying power:

	Req.	**Eq.**	
25% of M.V.	$25,000	$45,000	
		−25,000	
		20,0000	excess over maintenance
		× 4	requirements
		80,000	day trading buying power

Here is the account after the purchase of $80,000 of equity securities:

Market value	$180,000
Debit balance	135,000
Equity	45,000

If you recomputed the account at this point, you can see the account has utilized the maximum amount.

	Req.	**Eq.**
25% of 180,000	$45,000	$45,000

After the sale of the 80,000 in equity securities, the account will appear as follows:

Market value	$100,000
Debit balance	55,000
Equity	45,000

As you can see, the account is exactly the same as it started out. Since there was no increase in the customer's debit balance, there is no Federal or Regulation T call.

Time and Tick

Using the same example, once the customer is out of the position that he or she purchased, that customer can day trade another $80,000 of equity securities. Once out of that position, you can do it again and again. So at least in theory, you could day trade millions of dollars of equity securities in a day. You just must be out before going back in. That is referred to as *time and tick*—keeping track and making sure you are out of a position before going back in.

Regarding the $25,000 minimum equity requirement. The original requirement was that the $25,000 had to be deposited in the margin account prior to the customer day trading. However, broker/dealers may now use any settled and available funds, or any available market value from fully paid for securities, including money market mutual funds, held long in the customer's cash account to satisfy the $25,000 minimum equity requirement, without moving the funds or securities to the margin account. Broker/dealers must have adequate procedures in place in order to prevent the funds in the cash account from being used for other withdrawal purposes such as debit card and check withdrawals. Any funds, securities, or money market mutual funds held in the cash account cannot be used for the calculation of day trading buying power unless they have been moved to the margin account one business day prior to calculating the day trading buying power.

We are actually clarifying two things: (1) to meet the $25,000 minimum equity requirement, you can have the funds either in the margin or cash account; and (2) if it is in the cash account, it does not have day trading buying power. In order to allow day trading buying power, you would have to physically move it from the cash account to the margin account.

What happens when pattern day traders exceed their day trading buying power? In addition, to receiving a margin call, there are two penalties that apply. The account would have to be margin based on the two (2) times excess equity, rather than the four (4) times standard. In addition, use of the time and tick calculation would not be allowed.

The intent of this rule was to not create margin calls. The rule provides for four times leverage, and customers should only be trading up to that level. In the event a customer exceeds that four (4) times leverage provided, if the margin call is not met as required, aside from the two penalties just mentioned, the account should be restricted for 90 days to a cash-available basis until the special maintenance margin call is met. In an NYSE Interpretation Memo, it defined what *cash available* means. Cash available means 1 times Rule 431 excess, and no time and tick calculations will be allowed for accounts on a 90 day-trading restriction.

Broker/dealers may look to funds in a customer's cash account to satisfy a day-trade call without moving the funds to the margin account. This limited exception will only be permitted if the member organization has adequate procedures in place to prevent the circumvention of the two (2) day hold requirement on funds deposited into or held in that account. That is, the customer must be prohibited from using the funds for other withdrawal purposes such as debit card and check withdrawals relative to this balance while it is being used to satisfy the day-trade margin call. Funds deposited into the cash account within two business days prior to the creation of a day-trade call, which the member organization can utilize to satisfy the day-trade call, are subject to the two-day holding period following the close of business on the day of deposit.

When a customer of a member organization has multiple day-trade calls outstanding and the due date of the first day-trade call is still within the five business days, then the customer can meet the highest day-trade call amount. This will satisfy the remaining day-trade calls that are outstanding.

Day trading is a very sophisticated way of trading on margin and should be confined to professionals. Some brokers specialize in this method of trading, and their customers day trade exclusively.

CHAPTER SEVEN QUESTIONS

1. A customer sells short 100 XYZ at 50 and deposits the required margin. Sometime thereafter, the price of XYZ rises to 55. Show the account after the appropriate mark to the market:
   a. market value $5,500
   b. market value $5,000.
   c. credit balance $3,500.
   d. credit balance 0.

2. Fully paid-for customer's securities being held by the broker:
   a. may be commingled with those securities of the broker.
   b. must be segregated and identified as belonging to the customer.
   c. may be used by the broker for stock loans.
   d. may be hypothecated by the broker.

3. A purchase of a when-issued security is in a customer's cash account for $12,000. What is the requirement?
   a. $12,000
   b. $6,000
   c. $2,000
   d. $3,000

4. A when-distributed security is exactly the same as a when-issued security.
   a. True
   b. False

5. Customers' securities that are being held by the broker for safekeeping that were purchased in the customer's cash account may:

   a. be placed in bank loan.
   b. be used as collateral for a short sale.
   c. only be placed in segregation.
   d. only be used to support the broker's proprietary position.

6. The interest rate charged by the broker in a customer's margin account:

   a. must be paid directly to the broker.
   b. is charged by increasing the customer's debit balance each month.
   c. is charged annually.
   d. is based on the prime rate.

7. Initial purchase of a mutual fund in a margin account requires:

   a. 100%.
   b. 50%.
   c. 25% or $2,000, whichever is greater.
   d. are not permitted in the margin account.

8. Mutual funds purchased at one broker and then transferred into another broker may extend loan value in the amount of:

   a. no loan value.
   b. 50 percent.
   c. 75 percent.
   d. 25 percent.

9. As a result of a day trade in a restricted margin account, the customer lost $1,000. The customer would receive:

   a. an NYSE call for $1,000.
   b. a Reg. T call for $1,000.
   c. a Reg. T call for 50 percent, or $500.
   d. an NYSE call for 25 percent, or $250.

10. A pattern day trader is a customer that day trades four or more day trades in:

    a. three business days.
    b. five business days and represents 6 percent of the trade in that period.
    c. five business days and represents 3 percent of the trades in that period.
    d. a year.

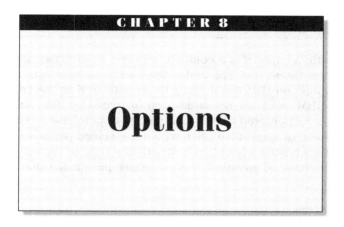

CHAPTER 8

Options

Options have been traded for well over 100 years. However, they did not actually become popular until 1973, when the Chicago Board of Trade formed a subsidiary called the Chicago Board Options Exchange (CBOE).

Prior to the CBOE, options were traded through put and call dealers. These dealers had a pool of investors who were willing to buy to accommodate sellers and sellers to accommodate buyers. Your broker would take your order to purchase 1 call option and go to a put and call dealer who, in turn, would go to their customers to see if someone would sell a call option on the particular security at the price stipulated and expiration date indicated, and the seller would charge a fee known as a premium.

As you can see, this was a very labor-intensive procedure. In addition, a physical call was issued and presented to the buyer. Although this system worked, volume was very low and there was virtually no secondary market. In other words, you could not sell the option. In the event it was profitable you had to exercise the option (buy the stock at the contract price and sell the underlying security in the open market, to obtain your profit). This all changed in 1973 with the advent of the CBOE.

Before proceeding, let's cover some definitions that you should be familiar with, because options have a language of their own.

DEFINITIONS

To begin with, an *option* is a contract between a purchaser and a seller, also known as the *writer*. The writer or seller actually creates the instrument. An option on IBM has nothing to do with IBM as the corporation. Options on IBM stock are not authorized or issued by IBM. An option is simply a contract entered into by two parties to purchase or sell a specified instrument, at a specified price within a specified period of time. The privilege of exercising any option is strictly the right of the purchaser. As with the purchase of anything, the purchaser pays a fee that the seller receives.

Options Issues

Equity: The underlying asset is a stock.

Broad index: The asset is a market index of multiple securities covering multiple industries' often called a broad-based index.

Industry index: The asset is a market index of securities of a particular industry, also known as a narrow-based index.

Interest rates: The assets are specific issues of U.S. Treasury bonds, U.S. Treasury notes or U.S. Treasury bills.

Foreign currency: The asset is a specific amount of a specified foreign currency.

Types of Options

Call: An option giving the holder the right to buy stock at a fixed price anytime during the life of the option.

Put: An option giving the holder the right to sell stock at a fixed price anytime during the life of the option.

Type: All listed options are either of two types, puts or calls.

Class: All options of the same type of the same underlying security; for example, all IBM calls (regardless of expiration months or strike prices) form the IBM call class. Puts on IBM would be a different class than IBM calls.

Series: All options of the same class with the same strike price and same expiration month; for example, IBM Apr 100 calls is a series of options and IBM Apr 110 calls form another series.

Spread: A simultaneous long and short position in different series of the same class. For instance, long 1 XYZ Apr 35 call and short 1 XYZ Apr 40 call would be a spread.

Straddle: A put and call (either both long or both short) on the same stock with the same exercise price and the same expiration month; for example, long 1 ABC Jun 40 call and long 1 ABC Jun 40 put.

Combination: A put or a call (either both long or both short) on the same stock, with either different exercise prices and/or different expiration months; for example, long 1 ABC Oct 30 call and long 1 ABC Oct 35 put.

Strap: One put and two calls of the same series, same underlying security, same expiration date, and same strike price.

Strip: The opposite of a strap. Two puts and one call of same underlying security, same expiration date, and the same strike price. Straps and strips usually can be purchased at premiums less than purchasing the options on an individual basis.

*Note: In our example of straddles, combinations, straps and strips, we used *long* positions; should an investor sell the options rather than go long (sell the positions), the investor would be *short* positions.

ADDITIONAL DEFINITIONS RELATED TO THE TYPES OF OPTIONS

Writer: The seller (creator) of an option position. The writer is often said to be *short* the option.

Opening transactions: Opening purchases create or increase long positions. Opening sales create or increase short positions.

Closing transactions: Closing purchases reduce or eliminate short positions. Closing sales reduce or eliminate long positions.

Strike price: Often times referred to as the *exercise price*. This is the price per share the buyer of a call agrees to pay the seller, should the call be exercised, or the price per share the seller of a put option agrees to pay the buyer if exercised. Listed options have standardized strike prices—usually multiples of 2.50 or 5 points.

In the money
1. On a call, the current market price of the stock is higher than the strike price.
2. On a put, the current market price of the stock is lower than the strike price.

Out of the money

1. On a call, the current market price of the stock is lower than the strike price.
2. On a put, the current market price of the stock is higher than the strike price.

Intrinsic value: If the option is in the money, the intrinsic value is the difference between the market price of the stock and the exercise price of the option. For example, when XYZ stock is at 53, the intrinsic value of the XYZ Aug 45 call is $800, regardless of the actual market price of the option. Consequently, out-of-the-money options have no intrinsic value.

Premium: The amount the buyer of the option pays to the seller for the option.

Time value: Sometimes referred to as *net premium*, which is any portion of the option above its intrinsic value.

Aggregate exercise price: The strike price of the option times the number of shares in the contract, normally 100 (as a result of a 3-for-2 stock split the contract could be for 150 shares). Therefore, the aggregate exercise price of a XYZ Apr 80 call would be $1,200.

Open interest: The total number of contracts in a given class or series capable of being offset by closing transactions. In other words, either the total number of outstanding short positions or the total number of outstanding long positions (not the total of both). Open interest in a given series may be zero, or it may be in the thousands, depending on the activity and popularity of the underlying stock. There is no rule or regulation limiting open interest to the number of shares outstanding.

Covered: Calls are covered when the short option position is protected by a simultaneous long position in the underlying stock; a security that is convertible into the underlying security; and escrow receipt; a warrant plus any cash required for the exercise of that warrant; or a call with an equal or lower striking price and expiration date equal to or longer than that of the short call option.

Puts are covered when and only when the account is long, a put with a strike price equal to or higher than the short put and an expiration date equal to a longer than the short put option.

The writer (seller) is not considered covered if he or she is short the underlying security. No margin is required on the short put when the writer is short the security.

Uncovered: Often times referred to as *naked.* This is where the short options would not have the various items already mentioned that make the option covered.

When dealing with options, keep in mind that there are only two kinds of options, put and calls. All the definition of spreads, straddles, combinations, strips and straps are nothing more than various combinations of puts and calls. Further, there are only two kinds of positions. You are either long or short. Keep it simple, and don't get caught up or confused by fancy or strange terminology. Put or call, long or short.

EXAMPLES

The following are examples of the various option positions reflecting maximum profit, maximum loss, and the breakeven point. The following examples do not include commissions, which vary widely from broker to broker.

Long Call

Buy 1 ABC Jul 60 call at 4 400.

Breakeven point would be 64 per share of the underlying security. Simply take the strike price, which would be your cost. In other words, you contracted to purchase the stock at 60 per share. If the security was, in fact, selling at 64 per share, you could purchase it at 60, sell it at 64, giving you a $400 profit. However, the cost of the call (the option contract) was $400—consequently you broke even.

Any higher would be a profit, any lower would be a loss.

A quick way of determining your profit would be strike price 60 + premium 4 = 64. In computing any option, always consider the option to be exercised.

Maximum loss would be the cost of the cost of the option (the premium) $400.

The maximum profit, at least in theory, is unlimited (how high is up)? As a matter of information, I indicated when computing options consider them as exercised and this will help you in your computations. In reality, if the stock was selling at 70, the premium would be at least 10 plus whatever time value, depending on how far away the expiration date was. Let's assume the time value was 2, for a total premium of 12.

The holder of this call option could exercise the option and hold onto the stock and sell the security at some future time. However, the holder of the call could sell the call for 12 total amount 1,200. Cost of call is 4 or $400, for a nice profit of $800.

Keep in mind that commissions would have to be deducted to determine your true profit.

Long Put

Buy 1 XYZ Apr 110 put at 7 700.

As the holder of the put, you have the right to sell 100 shares of XYZ at 110, and for this privilege you paid a premium of $700.

Your breakeven point is 103. Simply take the strike price 110 minus the premium 7 = 103. Again, consider the option as exercised. You buy the stock in the open market at 103 and put it to the seller of the option at 110, yielding $700. However, you paid $700 for the put option; therefore, you broke even.

Maximum profit is $10,300. If the security went to zero (0), there is no cost to you. Put the stock to the seller of the option for $11,000 minus cost of option $700 = profit $10,300.

Maximum loss is $700, the cost of the option. If the option was not profitable at expiration, you would let it expire and your loss would be $700.

Sell an Uncovered (Naked) Call (Short)

Sell 1 ABC Jul 40 call at 3.50 350.

Breakeven strike price 40 + premium 3.50 = 43.50.

Remember that you are the seller of the option; therefore, you are receiving the premium of $350. Any higher, and you would sustain a loss. Any lower, a profit.

Maximum profit is the premium of $350. The writer of the option (seller) always wants the option to expire, thereby keeping the premiums.

Maximum loss is unlimited again; how high is up?

Sell an Uncovered (Naked) Put (Short)

Sell 1 XYZ Jul 50 put at 3 300.

Breakeven strike 50 – the premium 3 = 47.

Maximum profit is the premium received, $300.

Maximum loss is $4,700. Keep in mind that you are the seller of the put option. If the underlying security went to zero (0), the buyer would put the stock to you at 50, for a cost of $5,000. However, you received a premium of 300 net, loss 4,700.

Long Straddle

Buy 1 ABC Apr 65 call at 4 400.
Buy 1 ABC Apr 65 put at 2 200.

Your breakeven point on the call option is 71. The strike price is 65 plus the combined premiums of 4 + 2, so 65 + 6 = 71.

On the put side, it would be 59: Strike price is 65 minus the combined premiums of 4 + 2, or 65 − 6 = 59.

Maximum loss would be the cost of the straddle. Your premiums are $600.

Maximum profit is unlimited due to the call option. The put would expire worthless, but the price of the security could just keep going up.

Sell an Uncovered (Naked) Straddle (Short)

Sell 1 XYZ Jun 40 call at 5 500.

Sell 1 XYZ Jun 40 put at 4 400.

Your breakeven point on the call side is 49. Strike price is 40 plus combined premiums 9 = 49.

On the put side 31: Strike price is 40 minus combined premiums 9 = 31.

Maximum loss is unlimited. You are short a call option.

Maximum profit is 900. In the event the straddle expires, you are in the premium received $900.

Long Combination

Buy 1 ABC Jul 30 put at 1 100.

Buy 1 ABC Jul 35 call at 3.50 350.

Your breakeven point on the call side would be 39.50. Total premium is $4.50, plus the strike of 35 = 39.50.

On the put side 25.50. Total premium is $4.50, minus the strike of 30 = 25.50.

Your maximum loss would be $450, the total cost of the options.

Maximum profit is unlimited, because you are long a call option.

Sell an Uncovered (Naked) Combination (Short)

Sell 2 XYZ Aug 15 calls at 2 400.

Sell 2 XYZ Aug 20 puts at 5 1000.

Breakeven point on the call side is 22.

Strike price is 15 plus combined premiums 7 = 22.

On the put side, 13 is the strike price, because 20 minus combined premiums 7 = 13.

Maximum loss is unlimited because you are short an uncovered call.

Maximum profit is $1,400 total premium.

Note that there are two calls and two puts.

Bull spread call debit is also called a vertical spread.

Note that the strike prices are different.

Buy 1 ABC Jul 50 call at 4.50 450.

Sell 1 ABC Jul 55 call at 2.50 250.

The reason why it is called a debit spread is due to the fact that you are paying out more than you are receiving. Buy $450, sell $250, net debit is $200.

Your maximum profit on this spread is 300. If the price of the security increased to 60, your long call with a strike at 50 would have a profit of $1,000. However, you are short a call with a strike at 55—hence, a loss of $500, less the cost of the spread $200. Maximum profit is $300.

Maximum loss is $200, the net cost of the spread.

The breakeven point is 52. You take the net premium 2 and add it to the lower of the two strike prices 50 = 52.

The term *spread* refers to the difference in premiums paid and received in the simultaneous purchase and sale of two or more series in the same class of option. The spreader hopes that this difference will either widen or narrow as the stock price fluctuates and the options approach expiration. In other words, the spreader's goal is to make money on one side faster than it is lost on the other. The simultaneous long and short position reduces the risk of a straight long or short position. However, at the same time this strategy eliminates the larger profit potential associated with such positions.

Although there are numerous variations, most spreads may be classified as either credits or debits. In a credit spread, the option sold produces more premium than the cost of the option purchased. In a debit spread, the option purchased costs more than the premium received on the option sold. Credit spreads are profitable when the spread narrows or when both sides expire unexercised. Debit spreads are profitable when the spread widens or when both sides are exercised.

Perhaps another example will make this clearer.

Bull Spread Call Debit, Sometimes Called a Money Spread

Buy 1 XYZ Apr 60 call @ 8   800 Pay
Sell 1 XYZ Apr 70 call @ 4   400 Received
                                 400 Net Debit

The current market price of the underlying security is 64.

The maximum profit would occur when XYZ is at 70 or any higher price. At this price, the spread would have widened to $1,000. The long Apr 60, which cost $800, could be closed out at $1,000 for a $200 profit. The short Apr 70 will expire worthless for a $400 profit. Each side (leg) of the spread contributes to the total profit of $600. Note that the spread cannot produce more profit than $600 because every point XYZ rises above 70 produces a point of loss on the 70 call, eliminating each additional point of profit on the 60 call. Thus, the maximum profit is the difference between the striking prices less the cost.

The maximum loss is the $400 net debit if both options expire worthless.

The breakeven is 64. Again, add the net debit 4 to the lower call strike 60 = 64.

Bear Spread Call Credit

Buy 1 ABC May 55 call at 2.50	250
Sell 1 ABC May 50 call at 4.50	450

Keep in mind in figuring any option to consider what the results would be if exercised.

In the previous example, you purchased a call option and paid $250. You also sold a call option and received $450. Consequently, you received a net credit of $200.

Your maximum profit would be $200. Let's assume the price of the underlying security (ABC) falls to 40. You certainly would not exercise your long call at 55, and no one would exercise your short call at 50. Therefore, both options would expire and you would keep the premium received of $200.

However, if the price of ABC rose to 60, you would be called at 50 for a loss of $1,000. However, you would exercise your call at 55, which would reduce your loss to 500, less the premium received $200 for a maximum loss of $300.

Your breakeven would be 52, which would be net premium received 200 added to the lower strike price 50 = 52. If the price did go to 52, your long option at 55 would expire worthless. But you would be called on your short option at 50 which would be a loss of $200 less the premium received 200 = 0. You broke even.

Bull Spread Put Credit

Buy 1 XYZ Aug 35 put at 2	200
Sell 1 XYZ Aug 40 put at 5	500

In this example, your maximum profit will be the premium received $300 net. Your maximum loss would be $200. Again, just walk through the process of exercising the options. Assume the price of XYZ falls to 10 per share. You would be put the stock at 40 for a $3,000 loss, but you would put the stock at 35 for a $2,500 profit, netting out to $500 loss, reduced further by the premium received $300 = $200 maximum loss.

The breakeven would be 37. Your short put would be exercised against you at 40. You sell the stock at 37 = $300. The loss is offset by the premium received, $300. You broke even.

Bear Spread Put Debit

Buy 1 XYZ Dec 20 put at 4	400
Sell 1 XYZ Dec 15 put at 2	200

In this case, if both options expire worthless your maximum exposure is your net cost of $200. However, if the underlying security (XYZ) went to 10 per share, you would exercise your long put at 20 for a $1,000 profit. However, your short put at 15 would be exercised against you for a loss of $500, reducing your profit to $500. This would be reduced further by the net cost of the spread, $200, so $300 would be your maximum profit.

Your breakeven at 18 net cost of premium 200 minus the higher put strike price at 20 = 18.

Although there are many more strategies, some of which are very complex, the examples cited are the most common and most widely used.

REQUIREMENTS FOR THE PURCHASE AND/OR SALE OF OPTIONS

Purchases of options may be made in the customer's cash or margin account. Payment is required by the settlement date T + 3 business days. Payment must be received no later than the fifth business day, the same as securities. In addition, you can obtain an extension of time. However, listed options are cleared and settled through the Option Clearing Corp. (OCC). The OCC requires settlement by the broker/dealer participants the next business day and that requirement is passed on to the customer. While Regulation T requires T + 3, the industry practice is T + 1.

Purchases of options in a cash account require full cash payment. Sales of call options are permitted in a cash account if the account is long the same security or equivalent security (see *covered calls*).

If a customer sells a put option in the cash account, this would be permitted if the account had cash equal to the strike price or cash equivalents (*money market instruments*).

If a customer sells or writes a put option on 1 XYZ Nov 35 with a premium of $500, the requirement is $3,500. The premium received $500 plus $3,000 in cash for a total of $3,500. The equivalent would be government securities, negotiable bank CDs or banker's acceptance notes having maturities of 1 year or less, with a market value of $3,000 plus the premium of $500, for a total of $3,500.

The balance of this chapter will be the various option positions taken in the customer's margin account, along with examples and margin calculations. Keep in mind that the margin requirements used in this book are always the minimum requirements set by the various regulatory organizations. Many firms have higher requirements, with some having substantially higher requirements. In fact, there are certain brokers that will not deal with options at all.

The vast majority of options have a life of nine months or less, and these options have no loan value. In other words, the broker is not permitted to extend credit on a long position on any option expiring within nine months.

In April 1996, the board of governors of the Federal Reserve delegated authority to self-regulatory organizations to set option margin requirements with the approval of the Securities Exchange Commission. Effective January 2000 the SEC approved the recommendations of an industry committee to allow a maximum loan value of 25 percent of the market value on listed options having a maturity of more than nine months. These are *long-term equity anticipation options*, more commonly called LEAPS.

For OTC options the loan value is 25 percent of the in-the-money or the intrinsic value. Consequently, when both listed and OTC get to the point that their maturities are less than nine months, no loan value may be extended.

LONG-TERM EQUITY ANTICIPATION SECURITIES

LEAPS

As previously mentioned, the listing of equity options on exchanges began in the early 1970s. Since that time an increasing number of strategies that employ this product have been developed. In addition to creating bullish, bearish, and neutral positions, options can be used to protect existing long and short positions.

One drawback in the use of options has been their limited life. In the past, exchanges listed options with an approximate maximum of nine months until expiration. The time factor increased the risk to the option's holder, as with each tick of the clock, a portion of the option's value vanished.

This negative was reduced to some degree in 1992 when the Securities & Exchange Commission approved the listing of options with as much as 39 months of life before expiration. Referred to as LEAPS, these Long-Term Equity AnticiPation Securities are similar to the traditional shorter options in their trading methods and strategic applications, although the increased time factor does allow for some expanded uses.

LEAPS are available in both puts and calls, and allow investors to protect against a decline in a stock or to take advantage of an upward move for an extended period of time. They are more closely related to an actual position in the underlying security than the shorter options. The extended time provided by LEAPS will command a greater premium than on similar options of less duration, but the cost will still be only a fraction of the amount required to purchase the underlying security.

LEAPS Example

With IBM stock trading at $100 a share, the purchase of 100 shares would cost $10,000 (plus commissions).

At the same time, an IBM 100 call with four months until expiration was available for a premium of .30 ($30). However, an IBM 100 LEAPS with thirteen (13) months until expiration commanded a premium of 10 ($1,000). Purchase of the LEAPS would give the holder a call on the stock for over a year at a price of 10 percent above the current market price. As LEAPS are traded American-style, the holder has the right to exercise at any time prior to expiration.

Although LEAPS offer certain strategic advantages, they cannot be considered equivalents to a position in the underlying stock. They are issued with longer durations, but they do, in time, expire. There is a continuing erosion of the option's premium, which works against the holder. An additional factor for investors to consider is that option holders do not receive any dividends, while stockholders generally do receive quarterly payments.

All usual strategies are available using LEAPS. Long or short positions can be established as with the shorter contracts and straddles and spreads can also be created. The only distinguishing feature of LEAPS is the time factor.

Investors must weigh the advantages of using LEAPS as opposed to using shorter options and rolling them over as each expiration approaches. As options are not suitable for all investors great care must be exercised before their use.

The basic factors for the trading of LEAPS are as follows:

Trading Unit	100 shares per contract
Trading Hours	9:30 A.M. to 4:10 P.M. eastern time
Settlement	the underlying stock
Exercise	American style
Expiration	the Saturday following the third Friday of the expiration month

Let us return to our margin calculations on the various option positions.

Short Call Uncovered and/or Naked

Sell 1 XYZ Nov 40 call at 5 $500

If the price of the underlying security was 40 the same as the strike price of the short uncovered call option, it is said to be "At the Money." In other words, there is no intrinsic value.

The initial margin requirement is the premium plus 20 percent of the current market value of the underlying security.

Premium	$ 500	
20% of Current Market Value $4,000	800	
	$1,300	Requirement

Use the same short call, except the current market value of the underlying stock is 45, commonly called *in the money*. There is intrinsic value of $500, which will be reflected in the premium.

Sell 1 XYZ Nov 40 call at 8 $800

The margin requirement is:

Premium	$ 800	
20% of Current Market Value $4,500	900	
	$1,700	Requirement

Again, use the same short call option except the current market value of the underlying security is now 38. The call is referred to as *out of the money*. No one would exercise a call at 40 when the security is selling below the strike price. The option would now appear as follows:

Sell 1 XYZ Nov 40 call at 2.50 $250

Premium	$ 250	
20% of Current Market Value $3,800	760	
	$1,010	Requirement
Less $200 which is the out of the money	– 200	
	$ 810	Requirement

These requirements are initial requirements like securities. There are minimum maintenance requirements, which is the greater of 20 percent of the market value of the current market value of the underlying security, plus the premium less the out-of-the-money amount, or 10 percent of the current market value of the underlying security plus the premium, whichever is the greater.

Use the same short uncovered call option where the current market value in a security is substantially below the strike price, known as a deep-out-of-the-money call.

Sell XYZ Nov 40 call at 1.25 $125

Premium	$125	
20% of Current Market Value $3,000	600	
	$725	Requirement
Less Out of Money	–1,000	
	($275)	Excess or Credit

Or

Premium	$125	
10% of Current Market Value $3,000	300	
	$425	Requirement

Obviously, $425 is the greater; therefore, that is the requirement.

The same margin requirements apply to short uncovered or naked puts. The only difference is the *out of the money*.

On a short call, out of the money is when the current market value of the underlying security is more than the strike price. On a short put, *out of the money* is when the current market value of the underlying security is greater than the strike price.

Let's look at the same examples as before, only changing the option from a call to a put.

Sell 1 XYZ Nov 40 put at 5 $500

At-the-money current market value of underlying security is 40:

Premium	$ 500
20% of Current Market Value $4,000	800
	$1,300 Requirement

Out-of-the-Money current market value of the underlying security is 42:

Sell 1 XYZ Nov 40 put 2.50 $250

Premium	$ 250
20% of Current Market Value $4,200	840
	$1,090 Requirement
Less $200 which is "Out of the Money"	−200
	$ 890 Requirement

No one would exercise a put when the security is selling above the strike price.

The minimum maintenance on a put option is the same as the call.

A short straddle is the sale of a put and call with the same strike price, same expiration, on the same underlying security. The margin required on a short straddle is the option requirement on the put or call, whichever is higher, plus the premium on the smaller side.

Sell 1 XYZ Oct 70 call at 4.50	$450
Sell 1 XYZ Oct 70 put at 2.50	$250
Current Market Value of XYZ stock	72.50

Call calculation:

Premium	$ 450
20% of Current Market Value $7,250	1,450
	$1,900 Requirement

Put calculation:

Premium	$ 250
20% of Current Market Value $7,250	1,450
	$1,700 Requirement

The call calculation is higher than that of the put. Consequently, that is the requirement.

Call Requirement	$1,900
Premium on Put	250
Total Initial Requirement	$2,150

Therefore, an initial call would be sent for $2,150 less the premiums received of $700, or $1,450. If the customer had available SMA of $1,450, that amount would be charged to the SMA.

A reverse situation would be if a customer wrote or sold a combination that has the same requirements as a straddle.

Sell 1 ABC Oct 40 call at 3	$300
Sell 1 ABC Oct 45 put at 6	$600

Call calculation:

Premium	$ 300	
20% of Current Market Value $4,100	820	
	$1,120	Requirement

Put calculation:

Premium	$ 600	
20% of Current Market Value $4,100	820	
	$1,420	Requirement

Since the put requirement is higher, $1,420 versus $1,120, that is the figure to use plus the premium on the call.

Put Requirement	$1,420
Premium Call	300
	$1,720
Less both premiums received	−900
	$ 820

$820 would be the initial call again. If sufficient funds were available in the customer's, SMA that would be the amount charged.

Bull Spread Call Debit

This is where you are long a call and short a call or long a put and short a put on the same underlying security and the same number of shares. Usually the expiration dates are the same. However, in the event they are not, the long option is the put or call having an expiration longer than the short options.

Buy 1 ABC Jul 50 call at 4.50	$450	
Sell 1 ABC Jul 55 call at 2.50	250	
	$200	Net Debit

The initial margin requirement is the amount of the debit, $200. The maintenance requirement is also $200. In other words, the initial and maintenance requirements are the same. This makes sense, since the maximum loss would be $200, which has been deposited or charged to the SMA.

Bear Spread Call Credit

Buy 1 ABC May 55 call at 2.50	$250	
Sell 1 ABC May 50 call at 4.50	450	
	$200	Credit

The initial margin requirement is computed by taking the difference between the two strike prices, $55 - 50 = 5$, or $500, less the net premium received.

	$500
Less Net Premium	−200
Initial and Maintenance Requirement	$300

Again, the maximum exposure is $300 and that is your requirement.

Bull Spread Put Credit

Buy 1 ABC Jul 40 put at 1.25	$125	
Sell 1 ABC Jul 50 put at 7.25	725	
	$600	Credit

The initial margin and maintenance requirement is computed by taking the difference between the short and long strike prices, $50 - 40 = 10$, or $1,000, less the premium received.

	$1,000
Less Premium Received	−600
Initial and Maintenance Requirements	$ 400

Bear Spread Put Debit

Buy 1 ABC Jul 50 put at 7.25	$725
Sell 1 ABC Jul 40 put at 1.25	125
	$600 Debit

Your initial and maintenance requirements are the same. You must deposit or charge the SMA the net debit of $600, which is the maximum exposure.

As the security industry moved more and more into international investments, we came across a different type of exercising requirement on European options. Therefore, we have two different styles of exercising.

The American Style

The holder of the option may exercise at any time after its purchase until the expiration date.

The European Style

The holder of the option may only exercise the option at a specified time, which for the vast majority means it is exercisable only on the expiration date. This restriction would not limit the holder to selling the option at any time during the life of the option; the holder would just be unable to exercise it.

Thus far, we have discussed the more common strategies of equity options, which simply means the underlying item is a stock.

OTHER TYPES OF OPTIONS

Index Options

There are two types of index options. *Broad-based index options* is where the underlying instrument is an index of numerous securities in numerous industries. In the Narrow-based index, the underlying instrument is an index of securities within a particular industry.

Index options, like equity options, are issued and cleared through the Option Clearing Corporation (OCC). However, the major difference between equity and index options is the way the exercise is settled.

In the event a customer owned 1 IBM Jul 100 call and decided to exercise the option, the seller of the option would be obligated to deliver 100 shares of IBM at 100 per share for $10,000. By contrast, index options settle for cash.

The closing price of the index is established each day the same as stocks, using the last sale at the end of the day. An example will help clarify this method of settling. If a customer owned a Standard & Poor's 500 call with a strike price of $1,400, the exercise price would be $140,000 ($1,400 × 100 = $140,000). If the closing price of S&P 500 was $1452.85, the seller of the option would have to deliver to the owner $5,285, the difference between the strike price and the actual value.

With a put, again using the closing price $1,452.85 and a strike price $1,500, the seller of the put would deliver $4,715. The difference between the exercise price and the market value is $150,000 − $145,285 = $4,715.

While retail customers do, in fact, use index options, they are favorite tools of institutional customers and professional traders.

The margin requirements on short narrow-based index options is 20 percent of the market value plus the premium, less the *out of the money*, or 10 percent of the market value plus the premium, whichever amount is greater. The margin requirements method of trading and the outcome is similar to equity options. The only thing that differs is the manner in which the index option settles. Actual stock settles equity options, money settles index options.

The margin requirements on short broad-based index options is 15 percent of the market value plus the premium less the *out of the money*, or 10 percent of the market value plus the premium, whichever amount is greater. The reason for the reduced margin requirement on the broad-based index is due to the much greater diversification of the underlying index. Consequently, there is less risk to the uncovered (naked) seller.

Example:

Short 1 index Nov 1430 call at 8.75

Current market value 1,433.35 in the money

Margin calculation premium 8.75 × 100	$ 875.00
100 × 1,433.35 = 143,335.00 × 15%	21,500.25
	$22,375.25

Interest Rate Options

These are options where the underlying security is a direct obligation of the United States government. They are further defined as Treasury bills (short-term debt obligations), Treasury notes (medium-term debt obligations) and Treasury bonds (long-term debt obligations). The contract size for Treasury bills is $1,000,000 face value. Treasury notes and bonds have a $100,000 face value.

The margin requirement on Treasury bills having a life of 95 days or less is the premium plus .35 percent of the face value. Keep in mind that the contract size is $1,000,000. The requirement on Treasury notes and Treasury bonds is the premium plus 3 percent and 3.5 percent respectively. The minimum maintenance requirements on Treasury bills is the premium plus .05 percent of the face value for call options and .05 percent of the strike price for put options. The requirement for Treasury notes and bonds is the premium plus .5 percent of the face value for calls and .5 percent of the strike price for put options.

Currency options differ in contract size, depending on the value of the respective country's monetary unit versus the U.S. dollar. The British pound contract is 31,250 pounds.

Example:

Buy 1 XBP Jun 167.50 call at 2.20. The premium is quoted in cents per unit calculation.

Contract × Premium
31,250 × $.0220 = $687.50

The total amount of the premium, $687.50, is required.

On the short side, the initial requirement is 4 percent of the market value of all the foreign underlying currency, plus the premium. However, there is one exception—the Canadian dollar, which is 1 percent of the market value plus the premium, less the out of the money or 0.75 percent of the market value of the underlying currency plus the premium, whichever amount is greater. Listed below are the various contract sizes:

Currency	Unit of Tracking	Quoted in
Australian dollars	50,000	Cents per unit
British pound	31,500	Cents per unit
Canadian dollar	50,000	Cents per unit
European currency unit (euro)	62,500	Cents per unit
Japanese yen	6,250,000	1/100 Cents per unit
Swiss franc	62,500	Cents per unit

As previously mentioned, various option strategies with various combinations of puts and calls both long and short have given rise to various names identifying them. Many of these combinations have already been discussed and are the more common strategies. What follows are the more complex strategies and their respective margin requirements. All options described must have an American-style exercise feature.

Conversion

Long security

Short a call

Long a put

The short call and the long put must have the same strike price and same expiration date. The initial or Reg. T requirement is 50 percent of the current market value of the long stock plus the premium on the long put. The premium received on the short call may be used to reduce these requirements. The minimum maintenance requirement is 10 percent of the exercise price of the underlying security.

Reverse Conversion

Short security

Long a call

Short a put

Both options must have the same strike price and expiration date. The initial or Reg. T requirement is 50 percent of the current market value of the short stock plus the premium on the long call. The premium received on the short put may reduce this requirement. The minimum maintenance requirement is 10 percent of the exercise price of the underlying security, plus the out of the money. (The amount by which the exercise price of the put exceeds the current market value of the underlying security.)

Collar

Long security

Short a call

Long a put

The long put has a lower strike price than the short call. However, the same expiration applies to both options. The initial requirement is 50 percent on the long security and pay the premium on the put option. The premium received on short call may reduce the requirement. The minimum maintenance requirement is the lesser of 10 percent of the put exercise price, plus out of the money of the put, or 25 percent of the call exercise price.

Unlike the three previous options, conversions, reverse conversions and collars, which require an American-style exercise feature, the following require a European-style exercise feature.

Long Butterfly Spread

Two short options of the same series are offset by one long option of the same type with a higher strike price and one long option of the same type with a lower strike price—all the same underlying security, same expiration date, and index multiplier. The intervals between exercise prices must be equal. The initial or Reg. T requirement is the net debit. The minimum maintenance requirement is the same as the initial requirement of the net debit.

Short Butterfly Spread

Two long options of the same series are offset by one short option of the same type with a higher strike price and one short option of the same type with a lower strike price. They have the same security, same expiration date, and index multiplier. The intervals between exercise prices must be equal. The initial requirement is the aggregated difference between exercise costs of the options. Use the two lowest premiums when the spread is composed of calls and the two highest when composed of puts. The minimum maintenance requirement is the same as the initial requirement.

Box Spread Long

A box spread long is long a call and short a put with the same exercise price versus a long put and a short call with the same exercise price, but higher than the first pair of options. In addition, all the options must have the same expiration date. The initial or Reg. T requirement is the net debit. The minimum maintenance requirement is the same as the initial requirement—the net debit.

Box Spread Short

A Box spread short is long a call and short a put with the same exercise price versus a long put and short a call with the same exercise price, but lower than the first pair of options. Again, all options must have the same exercise date. Initial or Reg. T requirement is the aggregate difference of the conversion cost of the two sets of options. Minimum maintenance is the same as the initial requirement.

These seven option strategies are hedging strategies used primarily by hedge funds, professional traders and institutions to minimize risk on the down or up side of the market and can become very complex when there are a number of different positions in the same account.

ADDITIONAL DETAILS CONCERNING OPTIONS

Expiration date: All listed equity options expire on the Saturday after the third Friday of the assigned month at 11:59 P.M. Normally, this is the third Saturday of the month. However, in the event the first of the month is a Saturday, the Saturday after the third Friday will be the fourth Saturday of that month (trust me or check a calendar).

Payment: As previously stated, purchases of listed options settle at the Option Clearing Corp. the next business day. In addition, the cutoff time is 10:00 A.M.

Exercise: Should a customer exercise his or her option, an *exercise notice* is issued to the OCC between 10:00 A.M. and 4:30 P.M. However, on the last trading day before the expiration date, notices are accepted up until 5:30 P.M. As a point of information, OCC will automatically exercise any option .75 of a point in the money at the time of expiration.

Trading hours: The market for listed options is 9:30 A.M. to 4:10 P.M. each business day. Once again, there is an exception on the last trading day prior to expiration—the trading stops at 4:00 P.M.

Assignment: When a broker receives instructions from his client to exercise an option, the *exercise notice* is sent to the OCC whereupon the OCC will randomly select the broker that is short that position. That broker does not necessarily have to be the broker who originally sold that option. The exercised broker must now select which one of his customers that are short that option, to be assigned. The broker may choose one of two methods: (1) a random selection, or (2) a method known as *first in, first out* (FIFO). Whichever client sold the first option will be the first assigned. Either method is acceptable; however, the broker must be consistent.

Dividends: Cash dividends have no effect on the option contract. However, stock dividends and stock splits do. Even stock splits are easy if you have an option as follows: (1) ABC Nov 100 call and there is a 2 for 1 stock split. You would now have 2 ABC Nov 50 calls. This same adjustment is made for puts as well. A different situation arises when there is a split of stock dividend that is not even—for example, a 3-for-2 split. Consider the same example of 1 ABC Nov 100 call.

$$\frac{10,000}{150} = 66.66$$

You will still have one option, but it will be for 150 shares with a strike price of 66.66.

A word of caution: Options are not for everyone, and some positions are risky and can be very speculative. The Chicago Board Options Exchange publishes a booklet titled "Characteristics and Risks of Standardized Options." This booklet is required to be sent to any customers wishing to trade options. I would strongly recommend that those contemplating trading options completely familiarize themselves with the risks of trading options, due to their complexity. Additional questions with detailed answers follow this chapter. Don't get disappointed with getting a wrong answer. Options are tricky. They have their own nomenclature that takes time to get familiar with. So learn from your mistakes and persevere.

CHAPTER EIGHT QUESTIONS

(All questions assume no transaction fees or commissions.)

1. XYZ common stock is at 85 and XYZ Oct 90 puts are trading at $800. The premium is composed of:
   a. $800 of time value.
   b. $800 of intrinsic value.
   c. $500 of time value and $300 of intrinsic value.
   d. $500 of intrinsic value and $300 of time value.

2. Which of the following best describes a *class* of options?
   a. all put options
   b. all IBM calls
   c. all options on IBM stock
   d. IBM Jul 120 calls

3. Which of the following options is in the money?
   a. ABC Oct 50 puts of ABC stock at 55
   b. ABC Jul 45 puts of ABC stock at 45
   c. ABC Jul 50 calls of ABC stock at 47
   d. ABC Apr 45 puts of ABC stock at 43

4. Each of the following will cause an adjustment to the terms of a listed option contract EXCEPT:
   a. $0.45 cash dividend.
   b. 15 percent stock dividend.
   c. 3-for-2 stock split.
   d. distribution of one preemptive right per share.

5. With ABC at 35, which option is at parity?
   a. ABC Oct 35 calls at 5
   b. ABC Oct 35 puts at 5

    c. ABC Oct 30 calls at 5

    d. ABC Oct 30 puts at 5

6. A buyer of an ABC Oct 15 call for which she paid $250 *exercises* her option. What must she pay?

    a. $250

    b. $1,250

    c. $1,500

    d. $1,750

7. Which of the following positions is a *straddle*?

    a. long 1 XYZ Oct 50 call – short 1 XYZ Oct 60 call

    b. long 1 XYZ Oct 50 call – long 1 XYZ Oct 60 call

    c. short 1 XYZ Oct 50 put – short 1 XYZ Oct 50 call

    d. short 1 XYZ Oct 50 put – short 1 XYZ Jul 45 put

8. An investor buys 1 XYZ Aug 70 call at $500 and sells 1 XYZ Aug 80 call at $200. The investor will profit if, at expiration:

    I. the spread has *widened* to more than $300.

    II. the spread has *narrowed* to less than $300.

    III. XYZ is at any price higher than 73.

    IV. Both options are exercised.

    a. I only

    b. II only

    c. II and IV only

    d. I, III, and IV

9. A buyer of an XYZ Feb 90 call may *first* exercise it:

    a. immediately.

    b. the business day following purchase.

    c. five business days after purchase.

    d. on the first business day in February.

    Questions 10 and 11 refer to the following information:

    An investor buys 100 shares of ABC at 24 and simultaneously sells 1 ABC Jun 25 call for $200.

10. At expiration, ABC is at 30. The investor's profit is:

    a. $100.

    b. $200.

    c. $300.

    d. $600.

11. The investor suffers no out-of-pocket loss unless at expiration, ABC is no lower than:

    a. 22.

    b. 24.

    c. 25.

    d. 27.

12. The OCC selects the member to whom an exercise notice is assigned on a:

    a. largest short position first basis.

    b. last in, first out basis.

    c. first in, last out basis.

    d. random selection basis.

13. The Options Clearing Corporation settlement day is the:

    a. business day following the trade date.

    b. third business day following the trade date.

    c. fifth business day following the trade date.

    d. seventh business day following the trade date.

14. XYZ Corp. is paying a 50 percent stock dividend. What adjustment will be made to an XYZ Dec 60 call on *ex-dividend* date?

    a. None.

    b. The contract will then be a 150 share Dec 40 call.

    c. The contract will then be a 150 share Dec 60 call.

    d. An additional 50 share contract will be issued with a 40 striking price.

15. What is the loan value of a long listed option with an expiration of six months?

    a. 0

    b. 30 percent of the underlying stock's market value

    c. 30 percent of the option's market value

    d. 50 percent of the option's market value

16. A customer sells short 100 XYZ at 100 and simultaneously writes 1 XYZ Jun 110 put for $1,500. The option order should be marked:

    a. "opening sale, covered."

    b. "opening sale, uncovered."

    c. "closing purchase."

    d. "closing sale, short."

17. A customer with no position in ABC stock writes 1 ABC Sep 40 call for $700 when ABC stock is at 42. Presuming all minimum equity requirements have been met, how much additional cash must the customer deposit?

    a. $840

    b. $700

    c. $630

    d. $200

18. In a cash account an investor buys 100 XYZ at 37 and simultaneously sells 1 XYZ Mar 30 call for $900. If there is currently no credit balance in the account, how much money must the customer deposit?

    a. $2,000
    b. $2,800
    c. $3,700
    d. $4,600

19. A speculator sells 1 ABC Aug 70 put for $500. If ABC stock is then at 72 and the trade took place in a properly margined account, what is the required margin on this position?

    a. $1,740
    b. $1,580
    c. $1,380
    d. $1,140

20. On the last trading day in December, ABC stock closed at 48. Expiring ABC December 45 calls traded at $300 at the close of options trading. If a trader with a long ABC December 45 call neither closed his position nor notified the broker to exercise before the exercise cut-off time, the option:

    a. expires worthless.
    b. will be closed out by a closing purchaser prior to expiration.
    c. will be closed out by a closing sale prior to expiration.
    d. will be automatically exercised by the OCC.

21. Presuming the stock underlying the options is not owned by the customer, which of the following subjects the customer to potentially unlimited loss?

    I. uncovered call
    II. uncovered put
    III. long straddle
    IV. short straddle

    a. I only
    b. I and IV only
    c. II and III only
    d. II, III, and IV only

22. XYZ stock splits 2 for 1. What adjustments will be made to a customer's XYZ Mar 30 call?

    a. The option will become a 200-share Mar 15 call.
    b. The option will become a 200-share Mar 30 call.
    c. An additional 100-share Mar 15 call will be issued to the customer.
    d. An additional 100-share Mar 30 call will be issued to the customer.

23. With XYZ stock at 40, an investor sells 1 uncovered XYZ Aug 50 call for .0625. What is the minimum margin required?
    a. $406.25
    b. $606.25
    c. $806.25
    d. $1,606.25

24. Listed equity options expire on:
    a. the third Friday of the expiration month.
    b. the business day preceding the third Saturday of the expiration month.
    c. the Saturday following the third Friday of the expiration month.
    d. the last business day of the expiration month.

25. An XYZ October 60 put is adjusted to reflect a 3-for-2 stock split. After the adjustment, the option's premium is quoted at 3. What would the buyer of this put have to pay?
    a. $30
    b. $300
    c. $333.33
    d. $450

26. With ABC stock at 42, a trader buys an ABC Sep 45 call for $100 and 1 ABC Sep 45 put for $600. The trader profits if at expiration ABC at any price is higher than:
    a. 43 or lower than 36.
    b. 46 or lower than 39.
    c. 48 or lower than 35.
    d. 52 or lower than 38.

27. Which of the following is a spread?
    I. short 1 XYZ Oct 50 put – short 1 XYZ Oct 55 call
    II. short 1 XYZ Oct 50 put – long 1 XYZ Oct 55 call
    III. short 1 XYZ Oct 50 put – long 1 XYZ Oct 55 put
    IV. long 1 XYZ Oct 50 put – short 1 XYZ Jul 50 put

    a. I and II only
    b. II and III only
    c. III and IV only
    d. I, II, III, and IV

28. Each of the following transactions may be executed in a cash account EXCEPT:
    a. buy 100 ABC at Jun 45 – sell 1 ABC Jun 50 call.
    b. sell 1 ABC Jun 45 – deposit $10,000 U.S. Treasury bills.

c. buy 1 ABC Jun 50 call – buy 1 ABC Jun 50 put.

d. buy 1 ABC Jun 50 call – sell 1 ABC Jun 55 call.

29. XYZ stock is at 67. A trader with no stock position sells 1 XYZ Aug 70 call for 300 and 1 XYZ Aug 60 put for $100. If XYZ is at 65 on the expiration date of the options, the trader will realize a:

a. loss of $100.

b. loss of $400.

c. profit of $100.

d. profit of $400.

Questions 30 and 31 derive from the following information:

Presume all minimum equity requirements have been met. ABC stock is at 27 and an investor sells one uncovered ABC Sep 35 put for $900 in a margin account.

30. What is the minimum Regulation T margin requirement?

a. $250

b. $505

c. $1,035

d. $1,440

31. If the market of ABC then rises to 36 and the premium falls to $200, what is the new maintenance requirement?

a. $840

b. $820

c. $740

d. $620

32. A customer buys 1 SPX (S&P 500 index option) Feb 1450 call option when the index is at 1460 and the premium is 6. How much must the customer deposit?

a. $600

b. $2,500

c. $1,460

d. $1,450

33. The euro contract size is 62,500, and a Mar call option has a premium of .46. How much must the customer deposit to purchase this option?

a. $28,750

b. $2,875

c. $287.50

d. $28.75

Use the following information to answer Questions 34 and 35.
A customer:

Sells 1 XYZ Apr 60 call at 8 800
Buys 1 XYZ Apr 70 call at 4 400

34. What is the customer's maximum profit?
    a. $600
    b. $400
    c. $1,000
    d. $800

35. What is the customer's maximum loss?
    a. $1,000
    b. $400
    c. $800
    d. $600

Portfolio Margining

U p to this point, the margin requirements we have discussed have been established by the Federal Reserve (Regulation T), which are initial requirements of 50 percent of the current market value on either long or short positions. The self-regulatory bodies set the minimum maintenance requirements of 25 percent of the current market value on long positions and 30 percent on the short side, with higher requirements on low-priced securities (see Chapter 5 on short sales).

Portfolio margining uses a separate margin account commonly referred to as a *portfolio margin account*. Consequently, we have established two types of margin accounts. The other that we have discussed in previous chapters is now referred to as a *Reg. T margin account*.

In a nutshell, the margin required in a portfolio margin account does not have a set requirement. The requirement is based on a risk factor that a customer can sustain on a particular position or positions in equity securities and in equity-related securities, namely options. In addition, portfolio margining will only be available on U.S. equity securities. All foreign equity securities will continue in the Reg. T margin account.

The result will, in most situations, be lower margin rates, since the computation will be tied to the risk factor of the actual portfolio. The proponents of this methodology were quick to point out that where positions are not hedged or where the account has a few positions and possible concentrations, the requirements will in fact be higher than the set margin requirements of Regulation T or the regulatory bodies.

Portfolio margining is not for everyone. Wall Street is taking a slow and cautious approach. As of this writing, many firms are not contemplating using portfolio margining. Those who are using it have restricted its use to large customers with sophisticated trading accounts.

The New York Stock Exchange (NYSE) has established a minimum equity of $100,000 (Reg. T margin account $2,000), and this is provided the broker/dealer has a very sophisticated intraday monitoring system with the ability to reprice the account throughout the day, to block trades, and so on. Accounts using the broker as a prime broker and executing trades away, the minimum equity is $500,000. All other accounts will be subject to a $150,000 minimum equity requirement.

A broker wishing to use a portfolio margin account for a customer must file an application with the designated examining authority (DEA), such as the NYSE or National Association of Security Dealers (NASD). The details are spelled out in Rule 431 for the NYSE and rules 2520 and 2860 for the NASD. There are a minimum of 19 detailed points of information that the self-regulatory organizations (SROs) require before their approval is given.

The day-trading restrictions in rules 2520 and 431 of the NASD and NYSE, respectively, will not apply if the portfolio margin account establishes and maintains a minimum equity of at least $5,000,000 and the broker has the ability to monitor the intraday risk associated with day trading. Portfolio margin accounts with equity of less than $5,000,000 are subject to the day-trading restriction previously discussed.

Since the margin requirements are based on risk, the SROs established the following definitions and requirements. The following is a portion of rule 2520 of the NASD:

> *(2) Definitions.—For purposes of this paragraph (g), the following terms shall have the meanings specified below:*
>
> > *(A) The term "listed option" means any equity-based or equity index-based option traded on a registered national securities exchange or automated facility of a registered national securities association.*
> >
> > *(B) The term "portfolio" means any eligible product, as defined in paragraph (g)(6)(B)(i) grouped with its underlying instruments and related instruments.*
> >
> > *(C) The term "product group" means two or more portfolios of the same type (see table in paragraph (a)(2)(F)(below) for which it has been determined by Securities and Exchange Commission (SEC) Rule 15c3-1a that a percentage of offsetting profits may be applied to losses at the same valuation point.*
> >
> > *(D) The term "related instrument" within a security class or product group means broad-based index futures and options*

on broad-based index futures covering the same underlying instrument. The term "related instrument" does not include security futures products.

(E) The term "security class" refers to all listed options, security futures products, unlisted derivatives, and related instruments covering the same underlying instrument and the underlying instrument itself.

(F) The term "theoretical gains and losses: means the gain and loss in the value of individual eligible products and related instruments at ten equidistant intervals (valuation points) ranging from an assumed movement (both up and down) in the current market value of the underlying instrument. The magnitude of the valuation point range shall be as follows:

Portfolio Type	Up/Down Market Move (High and Low Valuation Points)
High-capitalization, broad-based market index	+6% / −8%
Non-high capitalization, broad-based market index	+/−10%
Any other eligible product that is, or is based on an equity security or a narrow-based index	+/−15%

(G) The term "underlying instrument" means a security index upon which any listed options, unlisted derivative, security future or broad-based index future is based.

(H) The term "unlisted derivative" means any equity-based or equity index-based unlisted option, forward contract, or security-based swap that can be valued by a theoretical pricing model approved by the Commission.

(3) *Approved Theoretical Pricing Models.* Theoretical pricing models must be approved by the Commission.

(4) *Eligible Participants.* The application of the Portfolio Margin provisions of the paragraph (g) is limited to the following:

(A) any broker or dealer registered pursuant to Section 15 of the Exchange Act:

(B) any member of a national futures exchange to the extent that listed index options, unlisted derivatives, options on ETFs, index warrants or underlying instruments hedge the member's index futures; and

(C) any person or entity not included in paragraphs (g)(4)(A) and (g)(4)(B) above approved for uncovered options and, if transactions in security futures are to be included in the account, approval for such transactions is also required. However, an eligible participant under this paragraph (g)(4)(C) may not establish or maintain positions in unlisted derivatives unless minimum equity of at least five million dollars is established and maintained with the member. For purposes of this minimum equity requirement, all securities and futures accounts carried by the member for the same eligible participant may be combined provided ownership across the accounts is identical. A guarantee pursuant to paragraph (f)(4) of this Rule is not permitted for purposes of the minimum equity requirement.

It should be noted that a portfolio margin account is not permitted to have an accompanying special memorandum account (SMA) (see Chapter 4). That account is strictly associated with the standard Reg. T margin account.

As the rules require, positions must be separated into positions that are related with the same security or index. The firm must now revalue each related position for 10 equidistant upward and downward market price movements.

Upward Movement	Downward Movement
+3%	−3%
+6%	−6%
+9%	−9%
+15%	−15%

As you can see, manual calculations would be extremely difficult and labor intensive. Currently, the SEC has only approved one (1) particular system known as the *Theoretical Inter Market System*, more commonly referred to as TIMS. What the system does is take the 10 equidistant theoretical movements, compare it to the actual price, and determine the highest possible loss in the aforementioned parameters. That becomes the portfolio margin requirement.

The following examples are from the CBOE Web site Margin Calculator and OCC Web site CPM Calculator at www.cboe.com

Long 1,000 shares IBM at $100.00; short 10 calls IBM APR 95 at $7.70

Standard margin is $42,300.

Portfolio margin requirement is $10,000.

The standard margin requirement is 50 percent of the market value of $100,000, or $50,000 less the premium received on the short calls ($7,700). Thus, the standard margin requirement in this case is $42,300. Keep in mind that portfolio margin is based on risk, not loss. In the event IBM went to zero (0), the customer would have lost $42,300, not just $10,000. Consequently, this method of calculating requires a very sophisticated system to properly monitor price movements that change the risk factors.

Another example, say the customer is long 1,000 shares of IBM at $100; long 10 puts IBM APR 100 at $3.40.

Standard margin is $53,400.

Portfolio margin requirement is $3,400.

Standard margin is 50 percent of market value $100,000 = $50,000 plus cost of 10 put options at $3,400, for a total of $53,400.

Portfolio is only $3,400, the cost of the options. Again, if IBM went to zero (0), you could exercise your put option at 100. Your only loss would be the cost of the put options, $3,400.

This is a whole new concept, and only time will tell how good or bad this additional leverage is for the investor and the risk to the broker.

Here are just a few more requirements involving the mechanics of portfolio margining.

MARGIN DEFICIENCIES

In the event of a margin deficiency in a portfolio margin account, the deficiency must be satisfied within three (3) business days by the deposit of additional funds and/or securities, or by the establishment of a hedge that would reduce the margin requirements. Should the deficiency not be satisfied after three (3) business days, the broker is required to liquidate sufficient positions to eliminate the deficiency. Brokers are not permitted to allow eligible participants to make it a practice of liquidations to meet a portfolio margin deficiency. However, liquidations to eliminate deficiencies caused solely by adverse market movements may be disregarded.

As a matter of information, if a customer has a deficiency in the portfolio margin account but there is sufficient excess in the standard Reg. T margin account to meet that deficiency, the excess funds must be transferred to the portfolio margin account. However, a firm may use any excess funds in the portfolio margin account to meet a minimum maintenance call in the standard Reg. T account without transferring the funds.

Since this subject is so new, rather than have a quiz or test, I have taken a number of questions raised by the industry, along with the answers provided by the industry regulators.

CHAPTER 9 QUESTIONS

Eligible/Hedged/Unhedged Positions

1. Do unhedged positions need to be removed from a portfolio margin account?
2. How are money market funds treated in a portfolio margin account?
3. Are mutual funds considered eligible products for portfolio margin? If so, is there any distinction made between open-ended and closed-end funds in terms of one being allowable and the other not?
4. Are customers permitted to purchase fixed-income products in a portfolio margin account, in effect bypassing the standard margin account?
5. How would a non–margin-eligible equity security that is part of a hedge be handled in a portfolio margin account?
6. For restricted/control securities that currently require 40 percent (or more) under Rule 431, will those higher requirements still apply if those positions are carried in a portfolio margin account?
7. How are ETFs treated in the portfolio margin account?

Account Set-up

8. If a customer had a standard margin account and a portfolio margin account, whereby the legal name and the tax ID are the same, does collateral have to be transferred from the standard margin account to satisfy a margin deficiency in the portfolio margin account?
9. A firm is not planning to open new accounts for portfolio margin customers. Instead, it intends to take an existing margin account, isolate the eligible products from the noneligible products, and apply the appropriate TIMS and 431 requirements. Is this permissible?

Unlisted Derivatives

10. Since the only permitted option valuation model is the OCC's TIMS model, this seems to effectively make it impossible to include unlisted derivatives in a portfolio margin account since the OCC only provides option prices for listed options.

11. Would a purchase in a portfolio margin account of a long over-the-counter (OTC) option in an account that previously only had listed options, say for a $500 premium, trigger a $5 million minimum equity requirement, even if the client was charged (and paid) 100 percent of the purchase price of the OTC option?

12. Is an OTC derivative that has a non–margin-eligible security as its underlier eligible for portfolio margin?

Liquidations

13. Define liquidation.

14. How does a firm distinguish between deficiencies that arose due to market movements versus trading activity, particularly in the context of an actively traded account?

15. If the portfolio margin client closes out positions to meet a deficiency based on house requirements but the account is not below the TIMS requirements, would it be considered a liquidation?

The Federal Reserve

In discussing purchasing of securities on margin or credit, some background information on the Federal Reserve System is appropriate, since it regulates the amount of credit outstanding in the United States.

Most foreign countries have a central bank that is controlled by its government. The United States has a central bank, but it is not controlled by the government. In fact, parts of the central bank are spread throughout the country, as the United States has usually favored a decentralized type of control.

The Federal Reserve System is divided into 12 different districts throughout the country. If you look at the face of a dollar bill, on the left side you will see a large letter. This letter indicates which Federal Reserve Bank distributed the money, "A" is from Boston, "B" is from New York, and "C" is from Philadelphia. (A complete listing of the Reserve Banks with addresses can be found at the end of this appendix.) The Federal Reserve Banks do not print the money, they simply distribute it.

Remember that the Federal Reserve Bank is not a government agency. It is a bank, but a very special one. It is often called *the banker's bank*. Although there is no connection to the federal government, there is governmental influence.

At the top level of the Federal Reserve System is a board of governors. There are seven governors, and all are appointed by the president of the United States for a 14-year term. The only restriction on appointing a member to the board of governors is that no two governors may come from the same Federal Reserve district. In addition, since the terms are for 14 years, the governors are politically insulated from day-to-day pressures. The president normally appoints a governor every two years. Consequently, many members of the board are appointed by different presidents and political parties. Thus, many varying economic viewpoints are represented.

The level below the board of governors is a board of directors. Each of the 12 Federal Reserve districts has its own board of directors. Each board of directors consists of nine individuals, three of whom are appointed by the board of governors. However, the remaining six are elected by the member banks in each district. As you can see, two-thirds of each board is controlled by the member banks themselves. Each district also has a slate of officers.

We know that the primary purpose of the Federal Reserve is to regulate the amount of credit outstanding in the United States. Approximately 13,000 commercial banks are in the United States today. About 4,500 of these are members of the Federal Reserve System. How can a mere one-third of the banks be so powerful? These 4,500 member banks are responsible for 75 percent of the available credit in the United States.

How does the Federal Reserve control credit? There are three major ways and several less ways.

RESERVE REQUIREMENTS

As a member of the Federal Reserve System, a bank is required to maintain a percentage of its deposits at The Federal Reserve.

A bank has three basic types of deposits:

1. **D.D.A. or demand deposits accounts.** This is a fancy name for checking accounts. The bank has no idea when a customer is going to write a check or for what amount. For this reason, the monies in a customer's checking account require the highest percentage to be left with the Federal Reserve. There is a complex sliding scale formula, but for our use, the percentage is approximately 10 percent.

2. **Time deposits** (i.e., CDs) require a far smaller deposit, because the bank knows when it must return the borrowed funds and can make the necessary arrangements.

3. **Savings deposits** require about the same reserve as time deposits, because monies in savings accounts have a tendency to remain for longer periods of time than checking accounts. In addition, the bank has the right to require 30 days' notice prior to any withdrawal. This right is

seldom used, but it could become necessary if there were a *run* on the bank. Most people are unaware of this condition, but just read the first page of your passbook. As a member of the Federal Reserve, a bank is required to compute its reserve requirements daily. With the banking industry so highly computerized this task is easily completed.

If at the end of the day, the bank has a $20 million requirement, this is recorded and set aside until Wednesday. Wednesday is the end of the bank week. At this point, the member bank would look at its daily reserve requirement for the previous two weeks and take an average. If it came up with a requirement of $25 million, and there was only $15 million on deposit with Federal Reserve, it would have to deposit $10 million by the end of the day to be in compliance with the Reserve requirement. Under normal circumstances, it would be very difficult to attract sufficient deposits to satisfy the $10 million requirement. However, other member banks are making the same computation, and some will have excess funds. *Note*: No interest is paid on Federal Reserve deposits, which is one disadvantage in being a member of the Federal Reserve System. Since there is no advantage to leaving excess funds at the Federal Reserve, they become available to be lent to those banks requiring additional deposits. Hence, we get the term *Federal funds*, or, most commonly, *Fed funds*.

Members of the Federal Reserve have access to the Federal Reserve wire system, which can move funds from one bank to another in a matter of seconds. So, while the original meaning of Fed funds meant to meet the Reserve's requirements (and still does), Fed funds also have the broader meaning of immediately usable funds, as opposed to clearinghouse funds.

Clearinghouse funds are funds that the average person uses when writing a check to the landlord, the store owner, or a birthday gift. The funds are not usable by the recipient until the check clears. The check you wrote goes through the clearinghouse system, back to the originating bank, which moves the amount out of your account and into the account of the person to whom you wrote the check. If the banks are in the same Federal Reserve district, the check will usually clear the next business day. Checks between districts will take longer, depending on the distance between them.

The *Federal funds rate* is the amount one bank will pay another for the use of funds overnight. This rate is determined by supply and demand. If more banks require funds than have excesses, the Fed fund rate will increase. A classic example of this supply and demand function occurred on December 31, 1986, which also happened to be a Wednesday, the end of the banking week. On this particular day, the Fed fund rate hit a high of 25 percent and a low of 1/4 percent. This unusual situation was occasioned by the banks wishing to make some cosmetic changes in the balance sheet for the end of the year. However, the end of the year happened on a Wednesday, and because of these accounting moves, most banks found themselves buyers of Fed funds, which drove the rate to this unusually high rate. By the end of the day, when the banks had settled their requirements with the Federal Reserve, there was no demand for these funds, thus the drop to 1/4 percent.

With this brief background of reserve requirements and Fed funds, let us look at some of the main ways in which the Federal Reserve regulates credit in the United States.

Reserve requirements. If the Federal Reserve decided to increase the reserve requirement from 10 percent to 12 percent, this would be a very severe action. All member banks would come under the new additional requirement, and there would be no excess funds to borrow. To attract additional deposits, higher rates would have to be paid. If additional deposits were not attracted fast enough, *demand* loans would be called, causing liquidations, foreclosures, and so on. There is no doubt that increasing the reserve requirements tightens credit. The reverse, lowering reserve requirements, causes the member banks to have excess funds, thereby reducing interest rates and easing credit restraints. Tightening too much causes recessions; easing too much causes inflation. The Federal Reserve strives to strike a balance.

Discount rate. This is the rate the Federal Reserve charges it member banks to borrow money. The discount rate is historically lower than all other money rates, because the proceeds of the loan are restricted as to use. The member bank may only borrow at the discount rate if the proceeds are used exclusively for meeting the Federal Reserve's requirement. In addition, this loan is a secured loan. The Federal Reserve is willing to help a bank out and lend it money to meet its reserve requirements, but the loan must be collateralized by the very best securities—that is, Treasury bills, notes, bonds, or those issued by certain government agencies that are guaranteed as to principal or interest. Just recently, the Fed started allowing other types of securities such as CD's issued by banks to ease the credit crunch caused by the sub-prime mortgage debacle. Increasing or decreasing the discount rate has only a very minor effect on the amount of credit available.

Federal Open Market Committee. The actions and decisions of this committee have the most immediate effect on credit availability. Its effect in severity falls somewhere between increasing reserve requirement and changing the discount rate.

The Federal Open Market Committee (FOMC) comprises the 7 governors of the Federal Reserve board and 5 of the 12 presidents of the various districts throughout the country, one of whom is always the president of the Federal Reserve Bank of New York. The other presidents rotate on and off the committee periodically. This committee meets once a month (more often if needed) and decides the day-to-day credit policy that will be followed. Should the committee decide to tighten credit, this would be accomplished by selling various government obligations to the member banks and charging the banks' respective reserve requirement accounts. This would cause most banks to be below reserve requirements, and monies would then have to be found to replenish their account. Attracting additional deposits requires higher interest rates, which, in turn, means credit will cost the borrower more.

Now, if the FOMC decides that looser credit policies are in order, the Federal Reserve will start buying the various government bills, notes, and bonds and will pay the banks by crediting their reserve accounts. Then there would be excess reserves in the vast majority of the member banks. With no interest being paid on the funds left with the Federal Reserve, the member banks will withdraw the excess and put it in the hands of the public in the form of loans. To entice the consumer to borrow when there is a surplus of funds, the bank must lower its rate, and the competition must follow. When the FOMC buys, it eases credit and lowers interest rates. The Federal Reserve prefers this method to ease and tighten credit because it is readily reversible.

Other ways the Federal Reserve affects credit are related to the securities industry:

Regulation T: Regulates the amount of money a broker may lend on securities.

Table A.1 lists all of the margin requirements for equity securities, from inception to the current requirement of 50 percent.

The first margin requirement by the Federal Reserve was effective October 15, 1934, with a requirement of 45 percent having a two-step loan value rate of (1) 55 percent of the current market value or (2) 100 percent of the lowest market value from the past 36 months, but never more than 75 percent of the current market value. This cumbersome method stayed in effect until April 1, 1936, having a loan value of 45 percent on all equity securities.

TABLE A.1   History of U.S. Margin Requirements

Effective Date	Purchases
October 15, 1934	45%
February 1, 1936	55%
April 1, 1936	55%
November 1, 1937	40%
February 5, 1945	50%
July 5, 1945	75%
January 21, 1946	100%
February 1, 1947	75%
March 30, 1949	50%
January 17, 1951	75%
February 20, 1953	50%
January 4, 1955	60%
April 23, 1955	70%
January 16, 1958	50%
August 5, 1958	70%
October 16, 1958	90%
July 28, 1960	70%
July 10, 1962	50%
November 5, 1963	70%
June 8, 1968	80%
May 6, 1970	65%
December 6, 1971	55%
November 24, 1972	65%
January 3, 1974	50%

Short sales were not permitted until November 1, 1937. The margin requirements effective November 1, 1937, was 40 percent on long purchases (60 percent loan value) and 50 percent on short sales.

Effective February 5, 1945, the margin requirement was changed to 50 percent on long purchases, (50 percent loan value) and 50 percent on short sales. From that point on, whatever the requirement was on long equity purchases, it was the same for short sales.

Regulation U: Regulates the amount of money a bank may lend on securities.

Regulation G: Regulates the amount of money organizations other than banks and brokers may lend on securities.

There is an additional regulation, W, which at the direction of the board of governors, regulates minimum down payments on household

TABLE A.2 Federal Reserve Banks

District	Federal Reserve Bank	Address
1	Boston, Massachusetts	30 Pearl Street (Boston, MA 02016)
2	New York, New York	33 Liberty Street (Federal P.O. Station New York, NY 14240)
3	Philadelphia, Pennsylvania	925 Chestnut Street (Philadelphia, PA 19101)
4	Cleveland, Ohio	1455 East Sixth Street (P.O. Box 6387, Cleveland, OH 44101)
5	Richmond, Virginia	100 North Ninth Street (P.O. Box 27622, Richmond, VA 23261)
6	Atlanta, Georgia	104 Marietta Street N.W. (Atlanta, GA 30303)
7	Chicago, Illinois	230 LaSalle Street (P.O. Box 834, Chicago, IL 60690)
8	St. Louis, Missouri	411 Locust Street (P.O. Box 442, St. Louis, MO 63166)
9	Minneapolis, Minnesota	73 South Fifth Street (Minneapolis, MN 55480)
10	Kansas City, Missouri	925 Grand Avenue (Federal Reserve Station, Kansas City, MO 64198)
11	Dallas, Texas	400 South Akard Street (Station K, Dallas, TX 75222)
12	San Francisco, California	400 Sansome Street (P.O. Box 7702, San Francisco, CA 94120)

appliances, automobiles, and charge accounts. This regulation has not be applied since shortly after World War II. However, it is still on the books and was looked at during the years 1979 to 1980, when the United States was experiencing very high inflation.

Table A.2 lists the 12 Federal Reserve Banks and their addresses.

Customer Margin Account and SMA Sheets

Customer Margin Account

QUANTITY	SECURITY	PRICE	AMOUNT
		Market value	
		Debit balance	
		Equity	

SMA Account

DATE	DEBIT	CREDIT	BALANCE	EXPLANATION

Answers to Chapter Questions

CHAPTER ONE

1. b. By the fifth business day. While we would prefer the money to be received by the settlement date, the fifth business day is when payment must be received.

2. d. Any time a customer purchases a security and there is a sale of that security without full cash payment being received, that account must be frozen for 90 calendar days.

3. b. Ten business days after settlement is the latest that sold securities must be delivered to the broker.

4. a. The two requirements to use the extended payment for a C.O.D. transaction are (1) instructions of C.O.D. prior to the trade and (2) the reason for the delay, the broker's inability to obtain the securities for the delivery.

5. b. The Federal Reserve has given the power to grant extensions of time to the various exchanges and the NASD.

6. c. On the fifth business day after the trade date.

7. c. Full cash payment received within the fifth business day after the buy automatically lifts the 90-day restriction.

8. d. A *regular way* transaction means the trade settles on the third business day after the trade date.

9. b. The receiving broker must explain why he is DK-ing an item so that the delivering broker can take whatever corrective action may be necessary.

10. b. A cash trade settles at 2:30 P.M. of the trade date. Transactions done after 2:00 P.M. settle 30 minutes later.

CHAPTER 2

1. c. Excess over Regulation T may be withdrawn or converted into buying power, enabling the customer to purchase additional securities.

2. d. The debit balance is the amount of money the customer owes the brokerage firm.

3. c. When the margin requirements are at 50 percent, the loan value or the amount the broker is permitted to finance is also 50 percent. Should the Federal Reserve increase the margin requirement to 60 percent, the loan value would only be 40 percent.

4. b. Reg. T requires the Federal Call to be deposited no later than the fifth business day.

5. d. All of the ways indicated may be used to meet a margin call.

6. b. $7,500—50 percent of the market value = $20,000 minus the customer's equity of $27,500 = $7,500 excess over Regulation T.

7. c. Buying power at the 50 percent initial requirement is simply double the excess of $7,500, or $15,000.

8. b. When the equity in a customer's margin account is below the existing margin requirement, the account is known as restricted margin account.

9. b. $23,500. Any time there is a purchase in a customer's account, the market value and the debit balance are increased by the full purchase price.

10. d. Since there was no excess in this customer's account, a call will be for 50 percent of the purchase price, or $4,250.

CHAPTER 3

1. d. As indicated in the chapter, many firms have *house requirements* that are higher than the NYSE minimum maintenance requirement. Consequently, a request by the broker for additional funds due to a market decline is a maintenance call.

2. a. The NYSE minimum maintenance requirement is 25 percent of the market value of the long positions in the customer's account.

3. c. When the equity exceeds the requirement of the NYSE, this is excess over NYSE maintenance requirement. It may not be withdrawn or used as buying power. This excess simply means that the account may sustain even further market decline.

4. c. As previously mentioned, excess over NYSE equity may not be withdrawn.

5. d. Although the requirement for Regulation T is 50 percent, or $1,200, the NYSE initial requirement of $2,000, being greater, takes precedent.

6. b. 25 percent of the current market value is $4,500, the equity is only $4,100; therefore, the customer would be on call for $400.

7. a. To meet an NYSE minimum maintenance margin call by liquidation, the customer must sell four times the call of $400, or $1,600.

8. d. Purchases or sales without deposits or withdrawals do not change the equity in the customer's account. The account is better off percentagewise, but dollarwise remains the same.

9. a. When meeting a maintenance call by bringing in additional securities, you must bring in 4/3 of $750, which is $1,000.

10. c. Fifteen business days; this is the maximum amount of time.

CHAPTER 4

1. d. The primary purpose of the SMA is to preserve the customer's buying power.

2. a. Withdrawal of funds from the SMA will always increase the debit balance in the customer's margin account.

3. b. Monies deposited to meet an outstanding Regulation T call will not affect the SMA. Deposits not required for Regulation T will increase the credit in the SMA.

4. c. 50 percent of the current market value is the loan value of listed securities that may be placed in the customer's SMA.

5. d. Monies may always be withdrawn as long as the withdrawal does not put the account below the NYSE minimum maintenance requirement.

6. a. Credit the SMA $10,000. Although it is true that the customer's debit balance will be reduced by the $10,000 deposit, the debit balance is in the customer's margin account, not the SMA.

7. b. Credit the SMA $750. Since the funds were not needed for Regulation T purposes, a credit of $750 to the SMA would be proper.

8. c. A withdrawal from the SMA while the margin account is on NYSE call will only put the account on call further. No entry to the SMA; the request is improper.

9. a. Again, the money received was not required by Regulation T; therefore, a credit to the SMA would be proper.

10. d. The only time you could credit the SMA is when the excess is greater than the SMA balance—for example, if excess in a customer's margin account was $5,000 and the balance in the SMA was $3,000. In this case, a credit of $2,000 to bring the SMA equal to the excess would be permitted.

CHAPTER 5

1. d. All of the above statements are correct. You must be in a position to borrow the securities involved. In other words, you should not fail to deliver on a short sale. All sell orders must be specified as to either long or short. And last, in the event the security is listed on a national securities exchange, you are not subject to the up-tick requirement any longer.

2. b. The NYSE minimum maintenance requirement for securities selling below $5.00 per share is $2.50 per share or 100 percent of the market value, whichever amount is greater. In our example, the customer is short 1,000 of ABC at $1.00. The requirement is $2,500.

3. d. Regulation T says to treat the short sale as if it were long and release 50 percent to the customer. Consequently, there is no deposit required.

4. a. The covering of a short sale releases the 50 percent of the current market value. The short sale closed out at $7,500. Therefore, the customer may withdraw $3,750.

5. b. The NYSE requirement is $5.00 per share or 30 percent of the market value, whichever is greater. In this case, the 30 percent margin: 30 percent × $5,000 = $1,500.

6. a. $15,000—equity equals short market value—minus the credit balance: In our example, the customer would have two credit balances—one in the margin account, the other in the short account.

7. d. A restricted margin account. Short market value minus credit balance equals equity. Since the equity is below the 50 percent requirement, it is a restricted margin account.

8. c. Unlimited at least in theory. (How high is up?).

9. b. In this case, you are covered by the NYSE, and you are required to deposit $2,000, even if this puts the account in excess of Regulation T.

10. c. The customer is short 150 shares, by definition.

CHAPTER 6

1. d. 25 percent; listed convertible bonds are treated the same as listed equity securities.

2. d. A treasury bill is classified as an *exempt* security.

3. a. 15 percent of the market value or 7 percent of the principal amount, whichever is greater.

4. b. 98 percent of the market value.

5. d. All of the above are classified as exempt securities as defined by section 2(12) of the Securities Exchange Act of 1934.

6. b. 15 percent of the market value or 7 percent of the principal whichever amount is greater.

7. c. The next business day is the normal settlement date, although special arrangements may be made, such as two business days, etc.

8. b. 3 percent of principal or 6 percent of the market value, whichever is greater.

9. a. Foreign sovereign debt is to be treated the same as marginable corporate debt.

10. c. The ratings must be one of the two highest ratings, AAA or AA.

CHAPTER 7

1. a. Customer's margin account after the short sale and the appropriate deposit.

Margin Account	**Short Account**
$2,500 credit	Market value $5,000
	Credit balance 5,000

After the mark to the market:

Margin Account	**Short Account**
$2,000 credit	Market value $5,500
	Credit balance 5,500

The increase in the credit balance in the customer's short account was occasioned by sending the lender the additional $500 so that the lender of the securities would have 100 percent of the market value of the securities being loaned.

2. b. Must be segregated and identified as belonging to the customer.

3. d. $3,000. The requirement is 25 percent of the current market value or $2,000 whichever is the greater. 25 percent of $12,000 = $3,000 which is greater than $2,000.

4. b. False. A when-distributed security is in fact an issued security, just not distributed to the shareholders. However, it is in the process of being distributed.

5. c. Securities purchased in a cash account require full cash payment. Consequently, fully paid for securities must be placed in safekeeping or segregation.

6. b. The interest charged by the broker to a customer's margin account is done by simply increasing the customer's debit balance by that amount.

7. a. The purchase of a mutual fund is done directly from the fund itself. There is no secondary market. Therefore, it is considered a new issue requiring 100 percent. After 30 days, loan value may be extended.

8. b. As long as the purchase took place at another broker, the receiving broker may extend 50 percent immediately.

9. b. The loss of $1,000 would increase the debit balance by that amount since the account is restricted (no excess over Reg. T), a Reg. T or federal margin call for $1,000 must be issued.

10. b. The rule states four or more day trades in a five business-day period and those trades represent more than 6 percent of the total trades for that period, you are classified as a pattern day trader.

CHAPTER 8

1. d. A put is in the money when the market price of the stock is *lower* than the striking price of the option. The in-the-money amount is the intrinsic value of the option. An option is *out-of-the*-money has no intrinsic value. Time value represents anything in excess of intrinsic value in an options premium. In other words, the time value is a function of the option's duration and the relative volatility of the underlying stock. Thus, if a put is $500 in the money (90 strike, 85 market price), an $800 premium must represent $500 of intrinsic value and $300 of time value.

2. b. *Class* is defined as all options of the same *type* on the same underlying security. Because there are only two types of options (puts and calls), it follows that there are two classes of options on each underlying security (e.g., IBM puts form one class; IBM calls the other).

3. d. Calls are in the money when the market price of the underlying stock is *higher* than the striking price of the option. Puts, as described in Question 1, are in the money when the stock price is lower than the strike. Only (d) meets this test. When the stock price and the striking price are the same (b), the option is at the money.

4. a. *Any* form of stock or property distribution (including rights or spinoffs) causes an adjustment to the terms of a listed options contract. In some cases the cash value of a stock right is so small that the OCC may decide to make no adjustment in the option's striking price. This is decided on a case-by-case basis. On the other hand, no adjustment is *ever* made for cash dividends.

5. c. Parity for an option is the point at which, if the option is purchased and immediately exercised, the liquidation of the underlying security causes neither profit nor loss. In this example, an investor buys 1 ABC October 30 call for $500, exercises at $3,000 (total cost = $3,500) and sells the stock at $3,500. Net result = 0. Options tend to be at or near parity when in the money near expiration. In other words, the option has lost its time value and is trading at its actual worth (intrinsic value).

6. c. Unless adjusted for some distribution, *the aggregate exercise price* (cash necessary to exercise a call or put) is 100 times the striking price. Thus, $100 \times 15 = \$1,500$. The premium paid for the option itself has no effect on this account.

7. c. A straddle consists of a call and a put on the same underlying shares, each with the same striking price and the same expiration date. Both sides are purchased (long straddle) or sold (short straddle). The latter is illustrated in this problem.

8. d. The investor has created a *spread* position, a simultaneous long-short position in two different *series* within the same option class. As such options sell at different prices, the *difference* in premiums (cost to buy the long option vs. proceeds of short option) creates a spread. The spreader expects his difference to widen or narrow, depending on an anticipated price move in the underlying stock. In this case, the spread is placed at a debit (long side purchase price ($500) exceeds writing proceeds ($200), producing a $300 debit). *Debit spreads must widen to be profitable*. The maximum possible extent of this widening is the point at which *both options* may be exercised. This happens if

XYZ is higher than 80 at expiration, where the premiums will differ by $1,000, the difference between the striking prices. The breakeven point may be found by adding the debit to the lower striking price of a call spread. Thus, at 73 the $200 loss on the long call is offset by the $200 premium on the short call. Consequently, any higher prices must result in a profit on the overall position.

9. a. Listed options may be exercised *immediately* upon purchase. Care should be taken, however, to make sure a valid report of execution has been received from the exchange floor. Otherwise, the exerciser runs the risk of having exercised a nonexistent position.

10. c. If ABC is at 30 the call will be exercised and the investor will be paid the strike price (25) for stock that cost 24. To this $100 profit is added the option premium of $200, for a total profit of $300. At any price higher than 25, the underlying stock's value is irrelevant.

11. a. If ABC is at 22, and is sold at that price, the investor loses $200. At 22, however, the option expires worthless and the premium of $200 offsets the loss on the stock. At any lower price the investor suffers an out-of-pocket loss as the stock loss exceeds the premiums. This is referred to as the *breakeven point*.

12. d. With the exception of large exercises, the OCC selects a writer by a *random selection method*. Thus, the duration of an open short position is irrelevant to the likelihood of exercise. Put another way, an investor could write a call today and be exercised tomorrow, while a three-month-old short position in another account goes untouched.

13. a. Note that while Reg. T allows a customer five business days, members of the OCC must pay premiums or make security deposits on *the business day following the trade*.

14. b. Because this distribution is less than share per share (less than a 2-for-1 split or a 100 percent stock dividend), the contract is adjusted by increasing the number of shares and reducing the striking price proportionately. A 50 percent stock dividend is like a 3-for-2 split, meaning that 100 old shares will be worth 150 new ones. One then divides 150 shares into $6,000 (aggregate exercise price of the option) and arrives at a new striking price of 40.

15. a. Regulation T allows no loan value on a listed option with a life of less than nine months.

16. b. Short stock—short put position is not covered according to exchange rules. Although a stock price drop will not harm the writer of the put, a price rise exposes the position to *unlimited loss*. Because the word *covered* implies limited risk, the exchange only allows it to be

used with puts when the investor owns a put with an equal or higher striking price than the short put.

17. a. The required margin on uncovered options is found by adding the premium and 20 percent of the value of the underlying stock. If the option is out of the money, that amount may be subtracted. In this problem the call is in the money so the computation is simple: $700 (premium) plus 20 percent of $4,200 = $840, for a total *requirement* of $1,540. The question, however, asks for *deposit* (requirement minus the premium), hence $1,540 – $700 = $840 additional funds.

18. b. There is no maintenance margin on a covered call position so that the $900 premium may be applied to the cost of stock ($3,700 – $900 = $2,800).

19. a. $500 (premium) plus 20 percent of $7,200 = $1,440 for a total of $1,940, *less $200 out of the money* (put strike vs. market price 72) gives a total requirement of $1,740.

20. d. To protect against just such an occurrence happening by accident, the OCC automatically exercises a customer option expiring by .75 (or more) in the money. If a customer does not wish to exercise (typically because of commission costs and the risks in the underlying security position), his member firm instructs the OCC not to exercise.

21. b. Both positions I and IV contain a naked call, which is essentially a *short stock position*. In a long straddle (long a put, short a call), the loss is limited to the premiums. The worst that can happen with an uncovered put (II) is that the stock so purchased becomes valueless. This is possible but not likely—and even then it is far less risky than the unlimited risk of a short stock position. For example, an investor sells 1 XYZ Dec 20 put for $300. If exercised, the writer buys 100 XYZ at 17 ($2,000 less $300). Maximum possible loss is thus $1,700 if the stock becomes worthless.

22. c. The distribution is a 2-for-1 split. For any share-for-share (or greater) distribution, new 100-share contracts are issued at a reduced striking price. After adjustment the customer will have two 100-share XYZ Mar 15 calls.

23. a. The minimum uncovered margin may never be less than the premium plus 10 percent of the stock value. The computation used in Question 23 would produce a "negative" requirement: $6.25 + $800 (20 percent of $4,000) minus $1,000 out of the money. The minimum of premium plus 10 percent of stock value therefore applies: $6.25 + $400 (10 percent of $4,000).

24. c. Although important to OCC member firms, Saturday expiration is of little use to the customer. All customer positions must be offset or

exercised on the preceding business day (ordinarily the third Friday) for the investor to claim any value.

25. d. After adjustment, a previous XYZ Oct 60 put becomes a 150 share XYZ Oct 40 (see Question 14). Premiums are quoted in dollars and cents per share of the underlying stock. Thus, $150 \times \$3 = \$450$.

26. d. The trader has a long straddle. Breakeven points for straddles (or combinations) may be computed by adding the combined premiums to the call striking price and subtracting them from the put's striking price. With both strikes at 45 and the premiums totaling $700, the trader breaks even at 52 (45 + 7) or at 38 (45 – 7). At those points, the profit on the in-the-money leg offsets the loss on the expired counterpart. Any further rise or fall produces a profit.

27. c. A spread is a simultaneous long–short position in two different series within the same class (see Question 8). *Both* may be puts or both may be calls. Only choices III and IV meet this description.

28. d. This choice is a spread (see Question 27). Even though it is in some ways a *covered call*, it must be executed in a margin account because Reg. T requires such. Choice (a) is a covered call, (b) is a permissible cash-secured put, and (c) is a long straddle. Each is permissible in a cash account if everything is fully paid. In the case of the put, the T-bills adequately cover any potential exercise against the writer.

29. d. The position is a straddlelike vehicle called a short combination. If XYZ is at 65 upon expiration, *both* a 70 call and a 65 put will expire out of the money. The trader will have collected the $400 premium for his trouble.

30. d. Using previously given formulas (Questions 17 and 19), $900 (premium) plus 20 percent $\times$ \$2,700 = \$540, for a total requirement of \$1,440. Note that this is an in-the-money put.

31. b. Continuing from Question 30, $200 (premium) plus 20 percent of \$3,600 = \$720, for a total of \$920, less the \$100. The put is now out of the money.

32. a. Listed index options are the same as equity options. The cost is the premium 6×100 (the multiplier) for a total of $600.

33. c. The contract size $62,500 \times 0.0046$ for a total of $287.50. The Australian dollar, British pound, Canadian dollar, and Swiss franc are quoted in cents. Simply move the decimal two places to the left.

34. b. $400. This is a bear spread call credit. If both options expire, you keep the net premium.

35. d. $600. The difference between the strike prices is $1,000 less $400 premium received, or $600 maximum loss.

CHAPTER 9

1. No. Long/short positions will be subject to a valuation point range of +/– 15 percent. Customers will be expected to possess a certain level of sophistication. Approval will be required for uncovered options and security futures. In addition, firms will be expected to have risk-monitoring capabilities, which include the imposition of higher *house* requirements as well as various stress-testing scenarios and the ability to monitor concentrations of individual securities in a single account.

2. Money market mutual funds will be maintained at a requirement of 1 percent, provided the 30-day holding period is satisfied.

3. Yes; equity-based mutual funds or other products such as unit investment trusts and exchange traded funds (ETFs) are eligible for portfolio margin, provided they meet the criteria for margin eligibility under Regulation T.

    Open-ended, equity-based mutual funds are eligible for portfolio margin, provided the 30-day holding period promulgated under the Securities Exchange Act of 1934 is satisfied. Open-ended funds other than money market funds will be maintained at 15 percent. As a matter of information, currently the Option Clearing Corp. (OCC) cannot accommodate mutual funds but is working on it.

4. Yes. Fixed-income products can be held in the portfolio margin account but will be subject to conventional 431 minimum maintenance margin requirements.

5. A customer will not be permitted to obtain margin value from a non–margin-eligible security in a portfolio margin account.

6. Restricted/control stock will be maintained at 15 percent. However, only those shares that can be sold within a three-month period will be eligible for portfolio margin.

7. ETFs can be classified as high cap, non-high cap, or narrow based, depending on how OCC classified them. Therefore, they can be hedged against the securities in the index.

8. No. In this situation, the collateral does not have to be transferred. As long as the standard margin account has sufficient excess, the margin deficiency in the portfolio margin account can be considered met. However, as discussed with day trading, the SMA in the Reg. T margin account must be reduced by the amount of the portfolio margin deficiency.

9. Yes, provided the firm is able to identify the portfolio margin accounts and the positions eligible for portfolio margining. However, the firm

will have to provide to the exchange a file of all portfolio margin positions in the prescribed format in order for the exchange to isolate those positions that are margined under the TIMS methodology.

10. OCC's TIMS model can accommodate certain unlisted derivatives. If a listed security is the underlying and the terms of the option are similar to listed options, OCC should be able to price it. In other instances, firms would be required to have their proprietary pricing models approved by the SEC in order to effect transactions in unlisted derivatives. If contracts are more unique and custom tailored, the prices will have to come from the firm.

11. The exchange is currently making no distinction between long and short OTC options.

12. No. Non–margin-eligible securities are not permitted in the portfolio margin account. Therefore, any option or derivative based on that security will not be permitted.

13. Firms may not permit eligible participants to make a practice of liquidations to meet a deficiency, but liquidations to eliminate deficiencies caused solely by adverse market movements may be disregarded.

14. Firms that cannot distinguish between adverse market movements and new transactions should take a conservative view and apply the liquidation to all margin deficiencies.

15. If it can be determined that the deficiency was created as a result of a trade, the firm should apply the same rule set to house requirements.

Final Examination Questions

The following questions concern cash and margin accounts. The questions may be considered a final exam to test your understanding. Good luck!

1. Each of the following may be done in a cash account EXCEPT:

    a. buying a call.
    b. selling a "cash secured" put.
    c. buying a U.S. government security.
    d. selling short a listed security.

2. A customer makes a short sale of $1,800 of listed stock as an initial transaction in a newly opened margin account. What is the initial minimum NYSE requirement?

    a. $900
    b. $1,800
    c. $2,000
    d. $2,340

3. An investor buys 200 A Corp. at 50 in a margin account. If there is no SMA, which of the following deposits would properly margin the position?

    I. $5,000 cash
    II. $5,000 fully paid margin stock
    III. $10,000 fully paid mutual fund shares
    IV. $10,000 long call options held in the customer's cash account

a. I and II only
b. I and III only
c. II and III only
d. III and IV only

4. A customer's account has an SMA balance of $2,000. If the customer then buys $8,000 of listed securities, how much cash must she deposit?

a. $2,000
b. $3,000
c. $4,000
d. $6,000

5. A customer sells short 100 ABC @ 60 and makes the required Reg. T deposit. If ABC then rises to 65, the credit balance will be:

a. $2,500.
b. $3,500.
c. $6,000.
d. $9,000.

6. A customer fails to pay for a purchase in a cash account and the position is liquidated, *freezing* the account. Which of the following best describes this status?

a. the customer may not make any transactions for the next 90 days.
b. the customer may sell fully paid stock, but may not make purchases for the next 90 days.
c. the customer must deposit the full purchase price before entering any orders for the next 90 days.
d. the customer's account is closed and any remaining equity is returned.

Questions 7 to 9 refer to the following information:

A customer's margin account has the following positions:

Long Market Value	Debit Balance	SMA
$25,000	$13,000	$500

7. What is the customer's equity?

a. $500
b. $12,000
c. $12,500
d. $25,000

8. How much marginable stock may the customer purchase without depositing additional funds?

a. 0

    b. $250

    c. $500

    d. $1,000

9. If the customer sells $4,000 of stock, what will the SMA be after the sale (Ignore Question 8)?

    a. $500

    b. $1,500

    c. $2,000

    d. $2,500

10. On the same day, an investor sells $12,500 worth of securities and buys $13,200. If there were no SMA, a Regulation T call:

    a. would be issued for $350.

    b. would be issued for $700.

    c. would be issued for $6,600.

    d. would not be issued.

    Questions 11 to 13 refer to the following information:

    A customer's account has the following positions:

Short 200 A at 60

Short Market Value	**Credit Balance**	**SMA**
$12,000	$18,000	0

11. If the market value of A stock falls to $50/share, what is the customer's equity?

    a. $6,000

    b. $8,000

    c. $10,000

    d. $18,000

12. With A at 50, what would be the customer's SMA?

    a. $1,500

    b. $2,000

    c. $1,000

    d. $5,000

13. To what maximum level may A stock rise before creating an NYSE maintenance call?

    a. 63.50

    b. 65

    c. 69.25

    d. 78

14. A customer buys $10,000 of listed stock today in a margin account with no SMA. He will not receive a margin call if today he also does any of the following EXCEPT:

     a. cover a $10,000 short position.
     b. sell $10,000 of long stock.
     c. sell short $10,000 of a different listed stock.
     d. transfer $10,000 of fully paid stock from his cash account.

15. With no previous position, a customer buys 100 ABC at 30 and deposits $2,000 cash. If ABC then drops to 26, the investor:

     a. must deposit $200 in cash or securities.
     b. must deposit $400 in cash or securities.
     c. must deposit $400 in cash only.
     d. is not required to make further deposits.

16. An investor buys 100 XYZ at 120 and makes the minimum Reg. T deposit. How low may XYZ drop before an NYSE maintenance call is issued?

     a. 105
     b. 100
     c. 90
     d. 80

17. A customer's account status is as follows:

Long Market Value	**Dr**	**SMA**
$8,000	$5,700	$600

How much cash may the customer withdraw?

     a. 0
     b. $300
     c. $600
     d. $1,200

18. A customer's account has the following positions:

     Long Short

     Long 100 A at 40   Short 300 C at 9
     Long 100 B at 50   Short 100 D at 25

What is the minimum NYSE maintenance requirement?

     a. $3,550
     b. $3,810
     c. $4,260
     d. $4,500

19. A maintenance call may be met in any of the following ways EXCEPT:

    a. selling out long positions.

    b. depositing cash.

    c. depositing securities.

    d. applying an SMA balance to the call.

20. A customer's account is at 40 percent equity and has no SMA balance. If the customer sells $5,000 of listed stock, how much cash may she withdraw from the account?

    a. 0

    b. $2,000

    c. $2,500

    d. $5,000

    Questions 21 to 22 relate to the following information:

    A customer account has the following positions:

Long Market Value	Dr	SMA
$20,000	$7,000	0

Short Market Value	Cr
$17,000	$16,000

21. What is the equity?

    a. $12,000

    b. $20,000

    c. $29,000

    d. $37,000

22. If the customer covers the short position at the current market level, what will the equity be?

    a. $12,000

    b. $20,000

    c. $29,000

    d. $37,000

23. A customer wishes to withdraw $10,000 worth of listed stock from a margin account with a 40 percent equity. What minimum customer deposit would permit this?

    a. $2,500 cash.

    b. $2,500 in marginable securities.

    c. $5,000 cash.

    d. No stock may be withdrawn if the equity is less than 50 percent.

24. As an initial purchase in a margin account, a customer buys 100 ABC at $1,700. How much must be deposited?

    a. $850
    b. $1,700
    c. $2,000
    d. $2,850

25. Which of the following purchases would require the smallest margin deposits?

    a. 100M principal of XYZ Corp. 10s of 2010 – mkt price 90
    b. 100M principal of U.S. Treasury 11–1/2 – mkt price 101
    c. 100M principal of Flint Michigan 7's of 2015 – mkt price 93
    d. $100,000 XYZ Corp. 10 percent preferred stock – mkt price 100

Questions 26 to 28 refer to the following information:

A customer account appears as follows:

Long Market Value	Debit Balance
$16,000	$3,000

26. What is the customer's SMA balance?

    a. $3,000
    b. $5,000
    c. $8,000
    d. $13,000

27. How much buying power does the customer have?

    a.   0
    b. $6,000
    c. $10,000
    d. $16,000

28. If the customer used her buying power to its maximum extent, which of the following would correctly illustrate the account after purchase?

    a. LMV = $16,000 Dr = 0   SMA = $7,000
    b. LMV = $16,000 Dr = 3,000   SMA = $10,000
    c. LMV = $26,000 Dr = 13,000 SMA = 0
    d. LMV = $32,000 Dr = 13,000 SMA = $3,000

29. A customer has a credit balance of $5,000 in his cash account. On March 11, he places an order to buy 100 ABC. Having made no further deposits, he places an order to sell 100 ABC at 120, the current market level, on March 16. What should the registered representative do?

    a. Accept the order as instructed.

  b. Sell only the $5,000 worth already paid for in full.

  c. Sell only the $7,000 difference between market price and credit balance.

  d. Refuse the order.

30. A customer appears to have a bona fide reason for not being able to satisfy a Reg. T margin call within five business days. Who may grant an extension of the payment period?

  a. the registered representative

  b. the branch office manager

  c. the Federal Reserve

  d. the NYSE

31. A put option gives the holder the right to:

  a. buy 100 shares of the underlying security from the seller at the strike price.

  b. sell 100 shares of the underlying security to the writer of the option at the strike price.

  c. sell the put option in the market at the strike price.

  d. sell any portion of 100 shares to the writer of the option at the strike price.

32. A call option is in the money when the market price of the security is:

  a. the same as the strike price.

  b. higher than the strike price.

  c. the same as the strike plus the premium.

  d. the same as the strike price.

33. Before opening a portfolio margin account, approval must be obtained from which regulatory authority?

  a. SEC

  b. the Federal Reserve

  c. SIPC

  d. DEA

  Use the following information to answer Questions 34 to 36.

  A customer's margin account appears as follows:

Long	**Debit Balance**
100 ABC at 40 $4,000	
200 XYZ at 80 $16,000	$7,500

34. What is the equity in the account?

  a. $12,500

  b. $7,500

    c. $3,200

    d. $10,000

35. The SMA may be credited:

    a. $5,000.

    b. $0.

    c. $2,500.

    d. $12,500.

36. The buying power in the account is:

    a. $2,500.

    b. $0.

    c. $5,000.

    d. $12,500.

37. A customer's margin account is as follows with Reg. T at 50 percent. This account would be known as:

Market value	35,000
Debit balance	20,000
Equity	15,000

    a. portfolio margin account.

    b. account with Reg. T excess.

    c. restricted margin account.

    d. below NYSE minimum maintenance.

38. How much margin must the buyer of 1 ABC FEB 50 call at 6 have in a Reg. T margin account? Expiration is six months from trade date.

    a. 25 percent

    b. 40 percent

    c. 50 percent

    d. 100 percent

39. A buyer of a call option would have:

    I. limited risk.

    II. unlimited risk.

    III. protection against a short.

    IV. a leveraged position.

    a. I and II only

    b. I and III only

    c. III and IV only

    d. I, III and IV only

40. When a customer signs a *hypothecation agreement,* the customer is giving the broker the right to:

    a. sell out the customer.

    b. pledge the securities to finance the debit balance.

    c. demand the debit at any time.

    d. close out a short position at any time.

41. The purchase of a when-issued security in a customer's margin account requires:

    a. 50 percent.

    b. 25 percent or $2,000, whichever amount is greater.

    c. 100 percent.

    d. that the security be purchased in a customer cash account.

42. A customer who is short 100 shares of XYZ writes a 1 XYZ APR put at 4. The required margin on the put option is?

    a. the premium plus 20 percent of the current market of the underlying security.

    b. no margin requirement.

    c. the premium plus 10 percent of the current market value less the Out-of-the-Money.

    d. only the premium must be retained.

43. A customer receives dividends on a long position in his/her restricted margin account. The proper entry to the margin account would be?

    a. reduce the customer's debit by the amount of the dividend.

    b. credit the customer SMA.

    c. 50 percent of the dividend is a permissible withdrawal.

    d. reduce the debit balance and credit the SMA by the full amount of the dividend.

44. A nonpattern day trader's account is as follows:

Market value	10,000
Debit balance	5,000
Equity	5,000
SMA	0

What is the maximum amount this customer could day trade?

    a. $10,000

    b. $20,000

    c. $25,000

    d. $5,000

45. A customer makes an initial purchase in a *Just Opened Margin Account* of 100 ABC at 30 3,000. The Reg. T requirement would be:

    a. $2,000.

    b. $3,000.

    c. $1,500.

    d. $1,000.

46. Which of the following would have no effect on the customer's SMA?

    a. market appreciation

    b. cash dividends

    c. a voluntary deposit of cash

    d. a 10 percent stock dividend

47. Federal Reserve Board Regulation T applies to customer transactions of all of the following securities EXCEPT:

    a. U.S. Treasury securities.

    b. convertible bonds.

    c. listed options.

    d. listed warrants.

48. A customer sells short 500 XYZ at $56 per share. To protect his profit on XYZ, the customer should:

    a. buy 5 XYZ puts.

    b. buy 5 XYZ calls.

    c. sell 5 XYZ puts

    d. sell 5 XYZ calls.

49. Under Regulation T, the 90-day restriction or frozen account would apply to a customer who purchases and sells:

    a. different stocks in different accounts.

    b. stocks in different accounts.

    c. stocks in a margin account without fully paying for the purchase.

    d. stocks in a cash account without having first fully paid for the purchase.

50. A customer is exercised on an S&P index 695 put. The index closed at 680. The client who was exercised would:

    a. deliver cash.

    b. receive cash.

    c. deliver securities.

    d. receive securities.

1. d. Fully paid purchases and sales of fully paid securities are permitted in cash accounts. In general, any security that may be paid in full may be purchased. This includes all corporate stocks, bonds, and government and municipal securities. It also includes options *purchases* but prohibits *opening sales* except (1) "covered" calls; and (2) "cash secured" puts (choice b). In both cases, the risk is limited to the investment and the customer cannot become unsecured by an adverse price movement.

2. c. The NYSE's maintenance rules require a *$2,000* minimum dollar equity in any account established with either a debit balance or a short stock position. Although the full purchase price defines the maximum loss in an initial purchase, the short sale of $1,800 leaves open the possibility of unlimited loss.

3. b. Regulation T calls may be satisfied by deposits of: (1) cash equal to 50 percent of purchase price; (2) marginable stock equal to the purchase price; or (3) SMA balances equal to 50 percent of the purchase price. Mutual fund shares may also be used for such purposes. Long options (choice IV) have no loan value and may not be used to answer Reg. T calls, regardless of their market value.

4. a. SMA balances are applicable dollar-for-dollar against Reg. T calls. An $8,000 purchase generates a 50 percent Reg. T call of $4,000. Applying $2,000 SMA to this amount will require a $2,000 deposit of additional funds.

5. d. This is a bit of a trick question. Credit balances in short margin accounts (like debit balances in long accounts) are unaffected by price fluctuations. They change only through deposits or withdrawals of cash or securities. Thus, the credit balance created at the outset is still unchanged. Cr = short sales proceeds + Reg. T deposit = $6,000 + $3,000 = $9,000.

6. c. The 90-day "freeze" (or "block") is required under Reg. T. No customer order may be accepted until the customer deposits sufficient "good" funds (cash, cashier's check, etc.) or securities to cover the transaction. The block does not extend to the customer's margin account, or for that matter, to his cash accounts at other firms.

7. b. Equity = long market value less debit balance. $25,000 − $13,000 = $12,000.

8. d. With Reg. T at 50 percent, buying power for marginable securities is found by doubling the SMA number. Technically, it's the SMA divided by the current Reg. T requirement, thus, the doubling effect.

9. d. Even though the customer's equity is clearly less than 50 percent, a long sale will release 50 percent of the proceeds to the SMA. This amount will be added to any existing SMA balance. $4,000 × 50 percent + $500 (existing balance) = $2,500.

10. d. A sale of $12,500 versus a purchase of $13,200 generates a Reg. T call for 50 percent of the $700 difference, as if the owner had made an outright net $700 purchase. Reg. T, however, permits brokers to waive initial calls under $1,000 and the call required here is only $350 ($700 × 50 percent). Technically, the broker could demand the money, but standard street practice is to waive such calls.

11. a. Equity in a short margin account = Cr − SMV = $18,000 − $12,000 = $6,000.

12. c. With A at 50, the Reg. T requirement on 200 shares is $5,000. The equity is $6,000 (Question 11). Hence, the $1,000 excess over the current Reg. T requirement is posted to the SMA.

13. c. The NYSE maintenance requirement on short stocks (at prices higher than $17/share) is 30 percent. The price level at which the equity is so reduced is found by dividing the Cr by 1.3; $18,000 ÷ 1.3 = $13,846 short market value for 200 shares. Dividing this by 200 gives a per-share price of about 69.25.

14. c. The short sale creates another new position and requires another Reg. T deposit. Closing an existing position, however, releases money to the SMA. Thus, either a $10,000 long sale or short covering purchase will offset the Reg. T requirement generated by the $10,000 stock purchase. Other possible means of meeting a Reg. T call are: (1) deposit of

cash equal to 50 percent of purchase price; or (2) deposit of fully paid stock *equal* to the purchase price (choice d).

15. d. NYSE rules require a customer to demonstrate financial performance by establishing a $2,000 minimum equity before either borrowing money or establishing a short stock position. Once the investor has demonstrated this ability, no further margin requirements must be met on this original position (as long as the minimum 25 percent level is maintained), as it must be with any position. In this example, the customer's equity is $1,600 ($2,600 LMV − 1,000 Dr), but the customer is more than adequately margined with an equity of 61.5 percent.

16. d. After the prescribed Reg. T deposit is made the account appears:

$$\begin{array}{rl} \text{Long 100 XYZ at 12,000} & \text{LMV} \\ \underline{-6,000} & \text{Dr} \\ 6,000 & \text{EQ} \end{array}$$

The 25 percent NYSE level may be found by either: (1) multiplying the Dr by 4/3; or (2) dividing it by .75. If the market does fall to this level, the account appears:

$$\begin{array}{rl} \text{Long 100 XYZ @ 80} = 8,000 & \text{LMV} \\ \underline{-6,000} & \text{Dr} \\ 2,000 & \text{EQ} \end{array}$$

At this point, the $2,000 remaining equity is exactly 25 percent of the $8,000 market value.

17. b. Under normal circumstances, all of the SMA may be withdrawn in cash. The withdrawal of SMA, however, increases the debit balance and reduces the equity by like amounts. If all the SMA were to be withdrawn the account would be below 25%.

$$\begin{array}{llll} \text{LMV} & 8,000 & \quad & \text{SMA \$300} \\ \text{DR} & -6,000 \\ \text{EQ} & 2,000 \end{array}$$

After a $300 withdrawal, the equity would be exactly at the 25 percent NYSE maintenance level. Any further decline in M.V. would put the account on call. Any withdrawal of funds or collateral is prohibited if such withdrawal would reduce the investor's equity to less than 25 percent. The investor may therefore withdraw no more than $300 of the $600 SMA because this would reduce the equity to the minimum 25 percent level.

$$\begin{array}{ll} \text{LMV} & 8,000 \\ \text{DR} & -6,000 \\ \text{EQ} & 2,000 \end{array}$$

18. d. The customer's $9,000 long stock must be margined at 25 percent or $2,250. Short stock, however, presents a different problem, as the price of the shares determines the requirement. Hence, 300 C at 9 requires $1,500 (between $5 and $17/share. The requirement is $5/share). The 100 D at 25 requires 30 percent margin (share price over $17) or $750. The total requirement, therefore, is 2,250 + 1,500 + 750 = $4,500.

19. d. Maintenance calls require new deposits or position closeouts. An SMA balance may give a misleading appearance of safety. Because any withdrawal from the SMA will increase the debit balance, an account already in trouble will simply be worse off than before.

20. c. Even with an equity of less than 50 percent, the SMA balance is always increased by 50 percent of the sale proceeds and this may be withdrawn in cash.

21. a. Equity in a mixed (long and short) margin account may be found by two different methods. An easy, and logical, one is to total up account assets and subtract account liabilities. The assets are long stock and cash credits ($20,000 + $16,000 = $36,000). The liabilities are short stock and cash debits ($17,000 + $7,000 = $24,000). The equity is the difference between these totals, or $12,000.

22. a. To cover the short, the customer must purchase $17,000 worth of stock. The credit balance, by contrast, is only $16,000. The $1,000 shortage is made up by increasing the debit balance by that amount. After this transaction the account appears:

```
LMV   20,000
DR    -8,000
EQ    12,000
```

The dollar value of the equity has not changed, although one would now have an SMA balance.

23. c. Although it is rather unusual for a customer to withdraw stock from a margin account, "restricted" or otherwise, it may be done by depositing appropriate substitute collateral. This may be either marginable stock equal in value to the stock withdrawn or cash equal to 50 percent of the value of stock withdrawn. Of the given choices, only c satisfies this requirement.

24. b. A rather old (but still important) fact illustrates how an NYSE rule may override Reg. T. The NYSE does require a minimum $2,000 equity before a customer may borrow either cash or stock (see Questions 2 and 15). On a purchase, however, the customer cannot be asked to deposit more than the market value of that purchase, as this is the entire extent of his potential loss. If the $2,000 equity were already established, Reg. T's 50 percent requirement would prevail.

25. b. All except choice d are exempt from Reg T and thus need only meet NYSE maintenance levels. These are:

    a. nonconvertible corporate bonds, 25 percent of market value. In this case $90,000 × 25 percent = $22,500.

    b. U.S. government securities, 5 percent of principal amount; $101,000 market value, but $100,000 principal × 5 percent = $5,000.

    c. municipal securities, lesser of 15 percent of principal amount or 25 percent of market; $93,000 × 15 percent = $13,950 (25 percent is $23,250 and thus greater).

    d. preferred stock is subject to Reg. T at 50 percent; $100,000 × 50 percent = $50,000.

26. b. When no SMA balance is indicated in a question, it may be found (if any exists) by computing the account equity and comparing it with the 50 percent Reg. T requirement on the current market value. The equity is $13,000 ($16,000 LMV less $3,000 Dr) and Reg. T is $8,000 ($16,000 × 50 percent), meaning that the SMA balance is the $5,000 equity excess over the federal requirement.

27. c. With Reg. T at 50 percent, buying power is found by doubling the SMA (see Question 8). The customer may thus buy $10,000 of listed securities with no additional cash or securities deposit.

28. c. The full use of the SMA as buying power increases *both* market value of long securities *and* debit balance by two times the SMA figure. Hence, $16,000 LMV becomes $26,000 and $3,000 Dr becomes $13,000. At this point, of course, the account equity is exactly 50 percent.

29. a. The customer has 5 business days from the trade date, that is, until March 18, to satisfy Reg. T. The representative should accept the order, but the customer is still required to pay in full by March 18 at the latest. Reg. T does not allow for the paying out of "difference checks" for the amount that should have been deposited versus the proceeds realized. In this example, only the proceeds of the 50 shares actually paid for (by the existing credit balance) may be paid out. The customer will have to deposit another $5,000 and, in return, will receive the broker's check for $6,000.

30. d. The NYSE (or the designated examining authority, DEA) has the authority to grant extensions of time. It is not, however, an automatic approval, and the customer's excuse must satisfy the DEA before any extension is granted.

31. b. A put option gives the holder the right to put (sell) 100 shares of the underlying security to the seller (writer) of the option at the strike price at any time until the option expires (American style expiration).

32. b. A call option is in the money when the market value of the underlying security is higher than the strike price.

33. d. A broker wanting to open a Portfolio Margin account for a client must obtain approval from the broker's designated examining authority—NYSE, NASD, AMEX, etc.

34. a. The equity is $12,500. Market value minus the debit balance = the equity.

Market value	$20,000
Debit balance	7,500
Equity	$12,500

35. c. $2,500. The account has excess over Regulation T.

Req.	**Eq.**	
$10,000	$12,500	
	$10,000	
	$2,500	excess over Reg. T

Consequently, that is the amount that can be credited to the customer's SMA.

36. c. 5,000. The $2,500 represents excess over Regulation T. It may be withdrawn or converted into buying power of 5,000 at the 50 percent requirement—simply double the excess.

37. c. An account where the equity is below whatever the Reg. T requirement currently 50 percent is known as a restricted margin account.

38. d. Options with a life of nine months or less must be paid for in full in a Reg. T margin account.

39. d. The purchase of a call option gives the customer leverage because, for a limited time, you control the underlying security for a small amount of money (the premium). The risk is limited to the premium. If a customer is short, the underlying security and the price of the security increase. You can exercise the call option and close out the short.

40. b. The *hypothecation agreement* is an agreement signed by the customer that the securities in the margin account are not held in the customer's name and may be pledged to finance the customer's debit balance.

41. a. Purchases of when-issued securities in a margin account are treated the same as any issued security currently requiring 50 percent. Purchases in the cash account only require 25 percent or $2,000 whichever is the greater.

42. b. No margin is required. Since the customer is short the same security as the short put, the worst that can happen is the put is exercised against him. The security can be used to close out the short position. As far as the premium is concerned, it can be released to the SMA.

43. d. Since the money received (dividend) was not needed to meet a federal margin call, the proper entry would be to reduce the debit balance and credit the SMA by the full amount.

44. a. $10,000. After the purchase, the account would appear as follows:

Market value	$20,000
Debit balance	15,000
Equity	5,000

After the purchase, the account is right at the NYSE minimum maintenance requirement 25 percent × market value $20,000 = 5,000.

45. c. The Reg. T requirement is 50 percent of $3,000, or $1,500. However, the NYSE would require an initial requirement of $2,000.

46. d. Stock dividends would not affect the SMA. The market value of the security held in the account will be reduced by the value of the 10 percent dividend. You will now own 110 shares, but the market value will remain the same as the original 100 shares.

47. a. The Federal Reserve is empowered to establish margin requirements under The Securities Exchange Act of 1934. U.S. Treasury securities are exempt from this legislation. They are not included in the Federal Reserve's margin requirement.

48. b. As the customer is short the stock, he/she wishes to protect against an increase in price. The purchase of calls would accomplish this.

49. d. Purchases in cash accounts must be paid for in full at the time of sale. Full payment is not required in a margin account.

50. a. Settlement of index options are made in cash as the customer is being put at 695. When the index is trading at 680, the client must deliver cash equal to the difference in strike prices.

Glossary

accrued interest—The interest owed by the buyer to the seller of bonds because that individual held the bond for a portion of the next interest payment. Interest accrues up to, but not including, the settlement day.

ADR—American depository receipt. A receipt for foreign securities being held in the country of origin by a U.S. bank. This instrument facilitates the trading of foreign securities.

arbitrage—The purchase of one security and the subsequent sale of the same security, either long or short, to take advantage of the price spread in the marketplace.

baby bond—A bond with a face value of less than $1,000. The vast majority of bonds have a face value payable at maturity of $1,000. Most baby bonds are for a face value of $500.

bearer bonds—Bonds that are not registered in the owner's name. The holder is the owner. Since July 1983, any new municipal bond issued has to be registered. Although bearer bonds will eventually become extinct, a number of them are still around.

bond—An instrument representing debt by the issuer to be paid to the holder. Bonds are quoted as a percentage of par ($1,000). Therefore, a bond being quoted as selling at 80.5 percent of $1,000, or $805.

box—The *box* is an old term referring to the time when physical securities were held in the possession of the broker. There are now several boxes, such as active box, free box, and safekeeping (usually meaning the securities are held with the Depository Trust Clearing Corporation (DTCC).

business day—The best definition of a business day is one on which the New York Stock Exchange is open. This always causes confusion, since there are certain days that the banks are closed but the exchanges are open (Veteran's Day and Columbus Day). However, on Good Friday, the banks are open and the exchanges are closed.

buy-in—Occurs when securities have been purchased, but not delivered on time. The receiving broker goes into the market, buys the securities, and any loss is passed on to the firm failing to deliver the securities.

cage—The area in a brokerage firm where the securities are held, received, and delivered out. Years ago, as a security precaution, this area was literally was fenced off. Today, much more elaborate security devices exist.

callable—A feature of certain preferred stocks and bonds. This feature gives the issuer the right to call the security to redeem or retire the issue prior to the original maturity date. If bonds were issued when interest rates were very high, it would be prudent to issue callable bonds so they could be called, then refinanced if rates drop in the future.

call loan—A loan to be paid back upon demand by the lender. Brokers borrow money from banks at the broker's call rate, which is a secured demand borrowing.

cashiers department—A more refined term for the cage; the department responsible for movement of securities and monies.

cash on deliver—C.O.D. transactions are usually used by institutions to settle buy transactions. For example, ABC Pension Fund purchases 10,000 shares of IBM for $1,250,000 and issues instructions to deliver versus payment to ABC Pension Fund's bank. These movements are done through DTCC.

commingling—Mixing customer's securities that are fully paid for with those that are being financed. This is a violation of rules.

common stock—An equity security in a corporation representing an ownership interest and carrying rights such as the right to vote and share in the profits. These shares are easily transferable.

cover—The term used to describe closing out a short position, either by buying the security in the open market and returning it to the lender and/or delivering the long position against the short position.

credit balance—Free credit balance monies belonging to the customer. Ledger credit balance monies obtained as a result of the proceeds of the short sale and being used as collateral for the stock loan.

current market value—(1) The actual price paid when purchasing or received when selling securities. (2) When valuing securities in an account, it is the closing price of the previous day, as shown by any regularly published reporting or quotation service.

day trade—The purchase and sale of a security on the same day. There is no position in the security at the end of the day, either long or short; therefore, there is no initial Regulation T requirement.

debit balance—The amount of money the customer owes the brokerage firm.

delivery against payment—Regulation T description of a C.O.D. transaction.

discount rate—The rate at which the Federal Reserve will lend its member banks on a secured basis. The proceeds may only be used to meet the reserve requirement of the Federal Reserve.

discount window—The location where members of the Federal Reserve borrow at the discount rate.

don't know—DK is the term used when a broker or bank rejects a delivery of securities because the transaction is literally not known to the broker or bank.

down tick—The previous sale was higher than the present sale. For example, 10.50 10.37 the price 10.37 represents a down tick. If a customer wanted to sell short at this price, the short sale would be prohibited. Short sales of listed securities may be made only on an up tick or zero-plus tick. Certain selected securities are being tested without the up tick. Currently, there is a test being conducted allowing short sales on down ticks for certain securities. The test has been completed and the up-tick requirement for short sales has been eliminated.

equity—Represents the customer's ownership in the account. If the customer sold all the securities and paid all the debts, what would be left is the equity.

equity security—Represents ownership as opposed to debt. Common stock and preferred stocks are the most common equity securities.

excess margin—That amount of equity in an account above the amount required by the Federal Reserve for initial requirements or by the New York Stock Exchange for minimum maintenance requirements.

exempt securities—Direct obligations of the United States government—Treasury bills, notes, and bonds; obligations of agencies that are guaranteed as to principal and/or interest by the United States government; and obligations of any political subdivision of the United States (municipal securities). These are exempt from registration with the SEC and exempt from Regulation T of the Federal Reserve.

face value—The principal amount. The face value dollar amount payable at maturity for most bonds is $1,000.

fail to deliver—The selling broker does not deliver the security by settlement date to the buying broker.

fail to receive—The buying broker does not receive the purchased securities by settlement date from the selling broker.

Federal funds—Funds bought and sold by banks to deposit at the Federal Reserve to meet their reserve requirements.

Federal fund rate—The rate at which Federal funds trade. The variations are caused strictly by supply and demand.

Federal Reserve Board—Seven governors, all appointed by the president of the United States for 14-year terms.

Fed wire—One of the advantages of being a member of the Federal Reserve System is access to the Fed wire, which moves funds from one member bank to another member bank on the same day.

free funds letter—The letter that is required to be obtained when delivering purchased securities for payment from the receiving broker. It states that these funds do not represent the proceeds of the sale of that security.

free riding—Under Regulation T, it refers to purchasing a security and selling it prior to making full payment. This practice is prohibited.

frozen account—A cash account in which the customer has purchased a security and sold the same security without making full cash payment. During this frozen period (90 calendar days), purchases may be made only if funds sufficient for the full amount of the purchase are already in the account.

general account—The old terminology for a margin account. When Regulation T was revised in 1983, *general account* was replaced by *margin account.*

general obligation—A type of municipal security on which credit may be extended.

guaranteed account—Where one account is guaranteed by another for meeting the New York Stock Exchange minimum maintenance requirements.

house rules—Any rule by the broker that increases the requirements of the Federal Reserve or the New York Stock Exchange. For example, NYSE minimum maintenance requirements are 25 percent of the current market value. The broker may require 30 percent of the market value.

hypothecation agreement—An agreement signed by the customer that the securities in the margin account are not held in the customer's name and may be pledged to finance the customer's debit balance.

initial margin—Usually thought of as the initial requirement of Regulation T, which is currently 50 percent of the purchase price. Additionally, the New York Stock Exchange requires an initial margin of $2,000 to open a margin account.

listed stock—Any security traded on a National Securities Exchange.

loan value—The amount of money a broker may extend on marginable securities. The Reg. T requirement at this time is 50 percent; therefore, the loan value is 50 percent. If the Federal Reserve raises the Reg. T requirement to 70 percent of the market value, the loan value would be 30 percent.

long—Securities that are physically in the customer's account.

maintenance call—When a customer is notified that an amount of money must be deposited to maintain his margin account.

maintenance requirement—The amount of money necessary to maintain a customer's margin account. New York Stock Exchange requires a customer to maintain a minimum of 25 percent of the current market value.

margin call—A request for additional funds. It may be a maintenance call, or the initial requirement of the Federal Reserve.

margin department—The department in the brokerage firm that is responsible for maintaining the customer's account, ensuring compliance with the rules of the Federal Reserve, the Securities and Exchange Commission, the New York Stock Exchange, and the firm's own house policies (often called the credit department).

margin requirement—The initial requirement set by the Federal Reserve in Regulation T.

margin security—A security that a broker may extend loan value or credit on, including listed securities (meaning those traded on any national securities exchange).

mark to the market—Changing securities prices to reflect the current market values along with the appropriate debit or credit.

municipal securities—Securities issued by political subdivisions of the United States, better known as states, cities, counties, and towns. There are two types of municipal securities: general obligations and revenue bonds. General obligations are backed by the full faith and credit of the municipality. Revenue bonds are backed by the revenue generated by the particular facility. In the event the revenue is not sufficient to repay the interest or principal, the bonds go into default.

NASD—National Association of Securities Dealers. Founded in 1939 and granted authority to regulate its members and the over-the-counter market, similar to the authority the stock exchanges have in regulating their members and their markets.

nonpurpose loan—The old name for non-securities credit account. Revision of Regulation T in 1983 changed the name.

non-securities credit account—This account allows the broker to extend credit to a customer on a secured or unsecured basis if the purpose of the loan is for something other than purchasing or carrying securities;

for instance, the payment of taxes, purchasing a boat, or taking a vacation. Although the Federal Reserve allows 100 percent credit on securities, members of the New York Stock Exchange are only allowed to extend 75 percent loan value. The remaining 25 percent is the New York Stock Exchange minimum maintenance requirement. The NASD has a similar rule.

partial delivery—Delivery of only a part of the total shares bought.

plus tick—The current sale is higher than the previous sale. For example, 10.75 11, the price 11 represents a plus tick. Short sales of listed securities may only be made on an up tick or zero-plus tick, with exception of test securities (see *down tick*). The test has been completed and the up-tick requirement for short sales has been eliminated.

receive versus payment—Delivery of securities to a broker or agent who has been instructed to make payment upon receipt.

registered representative—A broker who is licensed to purchase and sell securities. He/she is registered to represent the brokerage firm.

registered security—Under Regulation T, any margin security. Under the Securities Act of 1933, any security that has been registered with the Securities Exchange Commission.

regular way settlement—The security settles three business days from the trade date.

regular way transaction—A security transaction done for regular way settlement.

Regulation G—Federal Reserve regulation that governs the amount of credit a non-broker or nonbank may extend on securities.

Regulation T—Federal Reserve regulation that governs the amount of credit a broker may extend on securities.

Regulation U—Federal Reserve regulation that governs the amount of credit a bank may extend on securities.

Regulation W—Federal Reserve regulation that governs the amount of credit that may be extended on things like household appliances.

rehypothecation—When a customer pledges securities to obtain a margin loan from a broker, the broker repledges them with a bank to finance the debit balance.

rejection—A delivery of securities is made versus payment and the delivery is turned down or rejected. Many times this is referred to as a DK. In reality, the DK is the reason for the rejection.

reserve requirement—The amount of funds that must be deposited with the Federal Reserve, depending on the size of the bank's demand deposit accounts, savings accounts, and time deposits.

restricted account—A margin account where the equity is below the existing margin requirement. For example, with the current requirement at 50 percent the following margin account would be restricted:

Market value	$10,000
Debit balance	6,000
Equity	4,000

retention requirement—The amount that must be withheld on the sale of securities in a restricted margin account (no longer a requirement).

revenue bond—A municipal security that will repay principal and interest as a result of the revenue generated by the particular facility.

safekeeping—Customers' fully paid-for securities or securities representing more than 140 percent of the customers' debit balance are kept segregated from all others.

securities loan—Securities that are loaned to facilitate a short sale.

segregate—See *safekeeping*.

settlement date—The date when securities are delivered in settlement of a sale, or the date money is due for a purchase. On most securities transactions, it is three business days after the trade date. On U.S. government obligations, the normal settlement date is the next business day.

short versus the box—The short sale of the securities that the customer is long, done for tax reasons or to lock in a profit or loss.

stock record—A record used by brokers to list the positions, locations, and owners of securities.

Treasury bill—A debt instrument of the U.S. government that matures in one year or less and is traded on a discount basis.

Treasury bond—Long-term debt instrument of the U.S. government from 10 to 30 years in maturity. Denominations run from $1,000 to $1 million.

Treasury note—Medium-term debt instrument of the U.S. government from 1 to 10 years in maturity. Denominations run from $1,000 to $500 million.

unlisted securities—Securities not traded on a national securities exchange, more commonly known as over-the-counter securities.

when-distributed—A security that is issued, but not yet distributed; for instance, if a company owns another company and is going to distribute the shares to its stockholders. Before the securities can be physically distributed, they may trade on a when-distributed basis.

zero-minus tick—A situation in which the previous sale is the same as the current one but is down from the last different one. For example, 10.50, 10.25, 10.25 the first 10.25 is a down or minus tick; the second 10.25 is a zero-minus tick.

zero-plus tick—A situation where the previous sale is the same as the current one but is up from the last different one. For example, 10.50, 10.67, 10.67 the first 10.67 is a plus or up tick; the second 10.67 is a zero-plus tick.

Index

Printed in the United States
By Bookmasters